THE BEDFORD

MW01136829

The English East India Company at the Height of Mughal Expansion

A Soldier's Diary of the 1689 Siege of Bombay with Related Documents

Edited with an Introduction by

Margaret R. Hunt
Uppsala University

and

Philip J. Stern
Duke University

Bedford/St. Martin's
A Macmillan Education Imprint

Boston • New York

For Bedford/St. Martin's

Vice President, Editorial, Macmillan Higher Education Humanities: Edwin Hill
Publisher for History: Michael Rosenberg
Acquiring Editor for History: Laura Arcari
Director of Development for History: Jane Knetzger
Developmental Editor: Kathryn Abbott
Editorial Assistant: Alexandra DeConti
Executive Marketing Manager: Sandra McGuire
Production Editor: Lidia MacDonald-Carr
Photo Permissions Manager: Jennifer MacMillan
Text Permissions Manager: Kalina Ingham
Permissions Associate: Chelsea Roden
Cover Design: William Boardman
Cover Art: © National Maritime Museum, Greenwich, London
Author Photos: (Hunt) Mikael Wallerstedt; (Stern) Duke Photography/Les Todd
Project Management: Books By Design, Inc.
Cartographer: Mapping Specialists, Ltd.
Composition: Achorn International, Inc.
Printing and Binding: RR Donnelley and Sons

Manufactured in the United States of America.

0   9   8   7   6   5
f   e   d   c   b   a

For information, write: Bedford/St. Martin's, 75 Arlington Street, Boston, MA 02116
(617-399-4000)

ISBN 978-1-4576-6401-4

Acknowledgments

Foreword

The Bedford Series in History and Culture is designed so that readers can study the past as historians do.

The historian's first task is finding the evidence. Documents, letters, memoirs, interviews, pictures, movies, novels, or poems can provide facts and clues. Then the historian questions and compares the sources. There is more to do than in a courtroom, for hearsay evidence is welcome, and the historian is usually looking for answers beyond act and motive. Different views of an event may be as important as a single verdict. How a story is told may yield as much information as what it says.

Along the way the historian seeks help from other historians and perhaps from specialists in other disciplines. Finally, it is time to write, to decide on an interpretation and how to arrange the evidence for readers.

Each book in this series contains an important historical document or group of documents, each document a witness from the past and open to interpretation in different ways. The documents are combined with some element of historical narrative—an introduction or a biographical essay, for example—that provides students with an analysis of the primary source material and important background information about the world in which it was produced.

Each book in the series focuses on a specific topic within a specific historical period. Each provides a basis for lively thought and discussion about several aspects of the topic and the historian's role. Each is short enough (and inexpensive enough) to be a reasonable one-week assignment in a college course. Whether as classroom or personal reading, each book in the series provides firsthand experience of the challenge—and fun—of discovering, recreating, and interpreting the past.

Lynn Hunt
David W. Blight
Bonnie G. Smith

Preface

The English East India Company at the Height of Mughal Expansion presents an exciting set of primary sources generated during a series of armed confrontations between the English East India Company and the Mughal Empire in the 1680s and early 1690s. The intention is to pique students' interest while at the same time reinforcing a number of key themes in global history. The documents presented in this book challenge the reader to consider multiple overlapping and conflicting forms of political power—whether wielded by merchant princes or by Mughal noblewomen, by East India Company bureaucrats or by pirates. That cultures were in constant flux during this period makes this diversity all the more challenging. This was a world of people on the move—from refugees to seafarers to bodies of men who lived by hiring themselves out to fight other people's wars. People spoke many different languages, worshipped a variety of gods, and followed a great array of customs. In this book, we present some of these people's own words to reflect the diversity along with the dynamism, the barriers to understanding and mutual sympathy, and the ways some people—often out of desperation—sought to traverse those differences.

The central document of *The English East India Company at the Height of Mughal Expansion: A Soldier's Diary of the 1689 Siege of Bombay with Related Documents* is the previously unpublished diary of James Hilton, an English East India Company soldier who lived through the 1689–1690 Siege of Bombay, an attack carried out by Sidi Yakut Khan, a tributary of the Mughal Empire. Having remained in manuscript until now, this diary tells us much about the day-to-day life of a soldier in a besieged town, techniques of seventeenth-century warfare and peacemaking, the multiethnic makeup of early modern South Asian ports, problems of loyalty and disloyalty, the ubiquity of disease and death, and the ways Europeans and South Asians both preyed on one another and sought to create working relationships. It also gives students access to a kind of manuscript source that would otherwise be unavailable to them, offering a rare opportunity to grapple with the many methodological issues historians face about the trustworthiness and verisimilitude of written records.

Supporting the diary (but not always in agreement with it) are a number of contemporary documents, written both by Europeans and by South Asians. These shed light on the origins of the 1685–1690 war between the East India Company and the Mughal Empire, revealing the English East India Company's mandate and operating procedures and introducing students to some of the key political and military features of the Mughal Empire. They also bring to life a wide range of people and personalities, from beleaguered East India Company employees to Indian coastal warlords, from deserting soldiers to a group of angry widows petitioning Parliament about the East India Company's exploitative policies toward its sailors.

We made special efforts, both in the Introduction and in the headnotes that accompany each related document, to place local events, both in South Asia and in England, within a larger global context. Containing as it does a number of archival documents, this book provides students with a unique resource for studying the complex history of South Asia at a time when the Mughal Empire was at the height of its power and the English East India Company was far from achieving the political hegemony it would later enjoy.

The appendixes contain a Chronology of the Siege of Bombay, a number of analytical Questions for Consideration that will aid students in interpreting the diary and related documents and enhance their overall understanding of the siege and its significance in world history, and a Selected Bibliography that provides suggestions for further research. Difficult terms, such as specialized South Asian maritime terminology, Persian military terms, the titles of Mughal officials, place names, and the like, are defined in gloss notes. Two maps help orient students to the places where these events occurred.

A NOTE ON THE SOURCES

For the manuscript sources presented in this volume, most spellings and capitalization have been modernized, and punctuation has been added, except in rare situations where we felt something about the original orthography far better expressed the meaning of the text. In the sources that had already been printed, we have generally kept the original spelling, capitalization, and punctuation unless we thought it would prove an obstacle to understanding, in which case we quietly changed it. We have generally regularized and modernized the spelling of proper and place names as well as administrative and legal terms, both English and South Asian, usually rendering them with the most common name in use today (if known), though in several cases, we have left the spelling or expression where we felt it captured something of the spirit or meaning of the original (well-known Anglicized South Asian terms are sometimes retained for example, usually with the original Persian or other word glossed in a footnote). On the whole, we have not italicized non-English words in the original documents; however, where the original source used italics for emphasis, we have often retained these. In cases where it is unclear if two sources were talking about the same person, we left the original spelling in place. Some of the translations have been modernized and infelicities of expression quietly altered. Dates are given in the old-style Julian calendar but with the year beginning on January 1.

ACKNOWLEDGMENTS

We would like to thank the following scholars for reviewing an early draft of the manuscript: Sumaiya Hamdani, George Mason University; Sean Kim, University of Central Missouri; Jyoti Mohan, Morgan State University; Shailaja Paik, University of Cincinnati; Haimanti Roy, University of Dayton; and Robert Travers, Cornell University.

We also want to thank our institutions, Uppsala University, Amherst College, and Duke University, for intellectual stimulation and research and travel grants that contributed to making this project possible. Andrew Ruoss, Ethan Mann, Ted Leonhardt, and Sam Kotz provided invaluable research assistance at various points in this process. We are also grateful to Bonnie Smith, who took an interest in our project and shepherded it through the early stages of the publication process. Special thanks go to Yael Rice, who discovered the image of Aurangzeb at a Chishti Shrine reproduced in these pages, translated the Persian inscriptions for us, and explained some of the aesthetic conventions of Mughal court painting.

At Bedford/St. Martin's, we thank Kathryn Abbott, Michael Rosenberg, Laura Arcari, Jane Knetzger, Arrin Kaplan, Mary Posman, Alexandra DeConti, Elise Kaiser, and Lidia MacDonald-Carr.

Margaret R. Hunt
Philip J. Stern

Contents

Maps and Illustrations

PART ONE

Introduction: The 1689 Siege of Bombay in Global Historical Perspective

In the early hours of the morning of February 15, 1689, Sidi Yakut Khan,[1] a coastal military commander with strong ties to the Mughal Empire, invaded Bombay, off the west coast of what is now India, and laid siege to the English East India Company's fort and settlement there (see Figure 1). The siege lasted almost a year and a half and led directly or indirectly to the death of much of the Company garrison and an untold number of townspeople, both European and South Asian. The conflict also left the town in ruins. As the English ran low on gunpowder, food, and money to pay the troops, a number of their soldiers deserted, and many ended up fighting for Sidi Yakut Khan against their former comrades.

The peace, when it came, was widely represented as humiliating to the Company and, by extension, a blow to English national honor. It became fodder for critics in England, who used it to argue that the Company was corrupt, greedy, violent, and poorly managed. This criticism in turn fueled nearly successful efforts to have the Company dissolved. Mughal officials, especially those in the nearby port town of Surat, also capitalized on the moment, using it to make demands on the Company for years to come. However, Company leaders saw or claimed to see the conflict as part of a larger strategy to assert themselves against both Asian and European rivals; to them, the so-called "War with the Great

1

Figure 1. *English Fort of Bombay,* 1672

This image of both the front (waterside) and back of "Bombay Castle," first printed in a seventeenth-century Dutch compendium of images and descriptions of coastal Asia, offers a sense of how contemporaries would have viewed the fort from both sea and land. It also shows the relatively incomplete state of the island's fortifications around the time of the siege.

Philippus Baldaeus, *A True and Exact Description of the Most Celebrated East-India Coasts of Malabar and Coromandel* (London, 1703). Photo © National Maritime Museum, Greenwich, London

Mughal" (or what some have come to refer to as the First Anglo-Mughal War) was hardly a failure. If nothing else, the long-term fallout from the war and especially from the invasion steeled the Company's resolve to build up both the civil and military infrastructure of Bombay—a move, one could argue, that set it on a path to transform that backwater settlement into a regional power and ultimately part of the backbone of the British Empire in India. One can also see in this incident the politics, society, and culture of early Bombay, and thus the faintest traces of the modern world city we now know as Mumbai. The Siege of Bombay was, in short, a regional conflict with global ramifications. It also tells us a great deal about the nature of the encounter between European and Asian empires in the early modern period.

Until fairly recently, the 1689 Siege of Bombay has gotten little attention from historians. One obvious reason is that the siege coincided with one of the most famous events in the history of the British Isles, the Revolution of 1688–89 (also known as the "Glorious Revolution"), which removed from power the Catholic king James II (Stuart) and replaced him with the Dutch Protestant William of Orange (crowned William III) and his wife Mary (crowned Mary II), who was also the daughter of James II. As a consequence, when British historians and English-language schoolbooks talk about 1689, they tend to focus on events in Europe and England, especially in London, as opposed to events happening half a world away. Nor is there much mention of the siege in the major Mughal memoirs and other sources that have been the foundation for much work on the reign of Emperor Aurangzeb. A second, more practical reason for passing over the Siege of Bombay is that it was so disruptive of the East India Company's governance in its Asian factories and settlements[2] that the usual flow of letters and reports to Company directors in London largely dried up. James Hilton's daily account of the siege is the only detailed source we have for this event, and it is being published here for the first time.

But the most important reason the Siege of Bombay has been neglected is that it does not fit well with the stories traditionally told about the English East India Company, British imperialism, and the nature of early modern Asian states and empires. The siege, which resulted from a much larger and more aggressive policy the Company had adopted across the Indian Ocean, challenges a long-standing vision of the seventeenth-century East India Company as a mere trader, which fell into its political ambitions almost inadvertently as a result of territorial expansion in the middle of the eighteenth century. Conversely, the conflict tests the assumption that the Mughal Empire and its greatest contemporary rivals, most notably the Marathas, were primarily territorial powers, with little interest in either sea power or commercial wealth. At the same time, the fact that the First Anglo-Mughal War was such a disaster for the English from almost its first day belies the triumphalist assumption that English imperial expansion—and, indeed, European expansion more generally—swept over the globe with the force of destiny.

THE NEW GLOBAL HISTORY

Today scholars are in the middle of a major reassessment of the way they think and write about global history, and this reassessment has been especially pronounced in relation to European encounters in Asia. There is a new emphasis on the contingent and unpredictable nature of European expansion and the many setbacks Europeans encountered.[3] Historians no longer study only imperial "successes" but instead see imperial expansion, in the words of Alison Games, as a "complex process, one riddled with trial and error, success and failure, triumph and despair."[4] Increasingly, historians also reject teleological assumptions about the motives and aims of people in the past. In the late eighteenth and early nineteenth centuries, a century or more after the events described in this book, the English East India Company conquered almost all of South Asia and came to dominate the Indian Ocean. But it would be wrong to assume that seventeenth-century Englishmen—or the seventeenth-century East India Company—aimed to do either of these things. This is not to say that the Company did not have political ambitions. However, owing to various factors—not least of which was the overwhelming reach and military power of the Mughal Empire—these took a much different form than they would one hundred years later.

Finally, historians today are more skeptical of the power of national or regional solidarities than they used to be. While an earlier generation of historians claimed to see both Europeans and Asians as unified constituencies, inevitably locked in combat (this notion is sometimes expressed in the contested phrase "clash of empires"), today scholars are more likely to point out the tensions and disunities within these groupings, not least among traders and settlers from Europe, as well as shifting relationships, alliances, and interactions that undermined the coherence of categories such as "European," "Asian," or even "English." This is often coupled with a stress on what historian Sanjay Subrahmanyam has called the "connected histories"[5] of Eurasia, meaning a kind of history that focuses not on incommensurability or inevitable differences but on the complex and shifting links, affinities, similarities, and conflicts among peoples, cultures, economies, and polities in early modern world history.

The Siege of Bombay lends itself well to all of these approaches. From the English perspective, it was a conflict ridden with despair and defeat. It also revealed a shocking degree of disunity among the European settlers, who in some cases were deeply hostile to the Company.

Even more disturbing, the Company found itself unable to rely on its own soldiers, many of whom fled to the enemy. At the same time, the fort was only able to hold out because of an alliance of convenience between the East India Company and the Maratha Empire, a growing power vying with the Mughals and others for regional dominance. The story of the siege thus puts center stage a dizzyingly entangled cast of characters—not just English, Mughal, and Maratha but also Portuguese, Dutch, Gujarati, Rajput, Abyssinian, Persian, and many others. This was global "connected history" of the most complex kind.

MUGHAL EXPANSION AND THE ENGLISH ACQUISITION OF BOMBAY

The defining political event of sixteenth- and seventeenth-century South Asia was the rise and expansion of the Mughal Empire. The Mughals[6] traced their origins from Central Asian, Turkic, and Mongol lineages of Timur (i.e., Tamerlane) on the one side and Chinggis Khan on the other. Emerging in the region around Kabul, the Mughals began their expansion into what is now northern India under Emperor Babur (1483–1530). By the time of the Siege of Bombay, under Emperor Aurangzeb, or Alamgir ("world-seizer") (r. 1658–1707), Mughal power had dramatically expanded, reaching almost to the southern tip of the South Asian subcontinent (see Map 1). Militarily this expansion relied on a combination of heavy—sometimes unworkably heavy—artillery and the mobilization of large armies supported by a nimble military labor market. Mughal power was also facilitated by a sophisticated and layered approach to governance that balanced the central authority of the emperor with a good deal of scope for local initiative. This was accompanied by a relative openness to ethnic and religious diversity. So, for example, while the Mughals themselves were Muslims and favored Islam, even under the self-consciously devout Aurangzeb the empire was adept at incorporating, co-opting, or ignoring both people and polities of various religious persuasions, including various forms of Hinduism. It was also multiethnic, welcoming courtiers, tributaries, and fighters of diverse origins and from many regions (Document 7).

It was this already remarkably cosmopolitan place into which Europeans sought to insert themselves in the early modern period. Of course, Europe had had commercial and military contact with Asia for centuries, from the campaigns of Alexander the Great to the travels of Marco Polo. The attempt to reach Asia by a maritime route was the holy grail

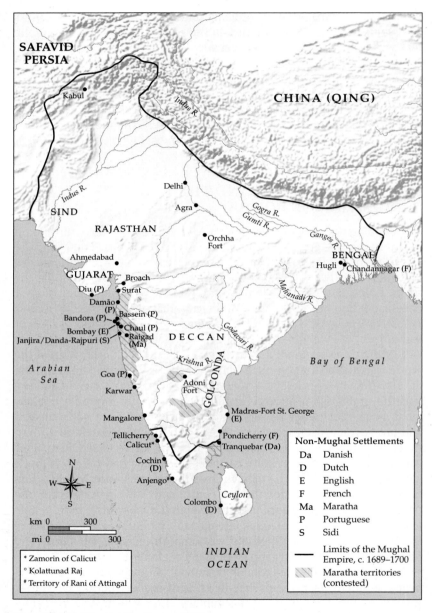

Map 1. *The Mughal Empire, c. 1689*

of fifteenth-century exploration; it was the original goal of Christopher Columbus in 1492 as well as many subsequent expeditions futilely seeking both a "northwest" passage (via what is now Canada) and a "northeast" passage (via what is now Russia) to the "East Indies." The arrival in India of the Portuguese explorer Vasco da Gama's fleet in 1498 and the subsequent founding of Goa on the southwestern coast of the Indian subcontinent, however, marked a significant change. Initially concerned less with the subcontinent than with the "Spice Islands" of what is now Indonesia, the Catholic Portuguese were, by the end of the sixteenth and beginning of the seventeenth centuries, challenged by other European competitors. Both Portugal and Spain had claimed a rather illusory dominion in the Atlantic and Indian Oceans based on a series of papal bulls (edicts) as well as the Luso-Spanish Treaty of Tordesillas (1494), which ran a line of demarcation near the Azores in the Atlantic, delegating responsibility for the western portions to Spain and the eastern portions to Portugal. Protestants, such as those from England, the Netherlands, and Denmark, as well as some Catholics (particularly from France) rejected this logic and began to undertake their own concerted efforts at maritime Eurasian trade by the beginning of the seventeenth century—fueled as well, perhaps ironically, by the massive influx of silver flowing to European markets from mines in Spanish colonial America and redirected into the trade to Asia.

Among these upstarts was the English East India Company, chartered in 1600 by Queen Elizabeth with the exclusive right among English subjects to trade with all of the lands and seas between the Cape of Good Hope and the Straits of Magellan. Its ships were heavily armed, though the main concern was not Asian polities but the Company's European rivals, especially the Portuguese Estado da India and the Dutch United East India Company (VOC),[7] itself created in 1602. The seventeenth century was marked by various and shifting alliances and conflicts among and between both European and Asian powers. From 1612 to 1615, the English East India Company, allied with Mughal forces, faced off against the Portuguese fleet at Suvali (known at the time to the English as Swally Hole or Swally Marine), which served as a deepwater anchorage for nearby Surat, the largest port and trading city in western India. Similarly, in 1622, the Company and the Persian (Safavid) Empire combined to force the Portuguese from the Persian Gulf port of Hormuz. In 1623, Dutch officials executed a number of English and Chinese merchants on the Indonesian island of Ambon, in what came to be known as the Amboyna Massacre, though not long after, an Anglo-Dutch alliance would seek to attack Portuguese interests in western India, including at Bombay.

Meanwhile, the English East India Company was attempting to create for itself more permanent settlements and a more secure trade in India. In the 1610s, the Company and the English king James I even sent an ambassador, Sir Thomas Roe, to the court of the Mughal emperor Jahangir; the Company's victories over the Portuguese fleet at Suvali helped Roe secure an imperial farman (imperial command or order) to establish its first factory (i.e., trading establishment) at Mughal-controlled Surat in 1616. Other factories soon followed throughout India. By the early 1640s, the Company had also obtained its own independent, fortified city of Madras (also known as Fort St. George) in southeastern India, similar in ambition to what the Portuguese had at Goa and the Dutch at Batavia (modern-day Jakarta in Indonesia). The Company had long desired something similar on the west coast of India where, unlike at Surat, it could be independent of Mughal authority. Such an opportunity arose in 1661. In that year, England and Portugal struck an alliance, sealed by the marriage of the English king Charles II to the Portuguese princess Catherine of Braganza. That treaty included the rights to two Portuguese settlements: the North African city of Tangier and the "Port and Island" of Bombay.

In fact, Bombay was not simply a port and an island but an archipelago of islands, marshlands, rivers, straits, and passages, which had mainly been under Portuguese jurisdiction and control since the early sixteenth century. Bombay itself was largely the private estate of a handful of Portuguese landowners. As a result, what precisely was meant to be transferred in the treaty would be a matter of conflict and controversy between the English and Portuguese for decades to come. Nonetheless, in 1668, the English government granted Bombay to the East India Company as a sort of colonial proprietorship, with full rights to make laws, punish offenses, govern its people, and organize military defense. Other prerogatives of sovereignty soon followed, such as the right to mint coin. The Company quickly set up a governmental infrastructure, especially during the tenure of Gerald Aungier, the island's third English governor (r. 1672–1675), creating, among other things, a system of courts and a series of fortifications around the archipelago. In 1687, it declared Bombay to be the center of its trading and political operations in western India, instead of Mughal-controlled Surat. Despite these efforts, Bombay itself grew slowly, its development complicated by environmental challenges; shortages of resources; high mortality rates; tensions with neighbors; and the need to build a civil society from a multitude of religions, ethnicities, legal systems, and commercial ties and interests. In the late 1680s, on the eve of Sidi Yakut

Khan's invasion, the Company's colony (as they called it) at Bombay was still very much an ambitious work in progress.

THE FIRST ANGLO-MUGHAL WAR IN REGIONAL AND GLOBAL CONTEXT

While part of the history of European expansion, the Siege of Bombay was in many ways also an extension of a much larger conflict raging over control and jurisdiction in western and southern India. During the latter part of the seventeenth century, Emperor Aurangzeb built upon the conquests of his Mughal predecessors by pushing decisively into western and southern India. In the process, imperial armies ran up against a number of other powerful sovereign polities, including Golkonda, Bijapur, the remnants of the Vijayanagar Empire, and, most famously, the Marathas. Maratha power had consolidated under Emperor Sivaji Bhonsle (r. 1674–1680)[8] in the 1660s and 1670s and quickly became a major threat to Mughal expansion. The result was a significant ramping up of conflict. Mughal expansion into Bijapur in the early 1680s, an area recently claimed by the Marathas, launched almost three decades of armed conflict—the so-called Deccan Wars (1680–1707)—that engulfed large parts of southern and western South Asia.

Often represented as contests over territory, the Deccan Wars also had a significant maritime dimension that is frequently overlooked. Both Marathas and Mughals extended their power to the sea, or at least to the littoral regions along the western Indian coast, which included the area around Bombay. However, this force was not represented by a navy as we might understand it today. Rather, it was constituted similarly to the way military service was on land; that is, through various forms of tributary, itinerant, and somewhat decentralized power. Mughal might along the Gujarati coast was primarily embodied in the Sidis, people of East African ancestry who had established themselves in South Asia over the course of the previous millennium. Initially coming to southern Asia as traders, laborers, and slaves, over the centuries Sidis had gained an enviable reputation as warriors and seafarers, and some had become quite prominent officials in princely households. By the mid-seventeenth century, perhaps earlier, a group of Sidis had established themselves as a semiautonomous power on the coast, based in the coastal fortified enclave of Danda-Rajpuri and the adjoining island fortress of Janjira.

In 1689, this principality was under the coleadership of Sidi Yakut Khan and another Sidi who may have been a relative. Sidi Yakut had earned the esteem of the Mughals through a series of notable victories against the Marathas. As a result, he was given a mansab[9] by Aurangzeb and, at some point, also acquired the honorifics Yakut and Khan. Khafi Khan's account (Document 8) suggests that Sidi Yakut was charismatic, extremely resourceful, and not a man to be trifled with.

As his jostling with Maratha power at sea became more heated, Sidi Yakut grew ambitious for control of the region. During the 1670s and 1680s, both Sidi and Maratha forces had attempted to take up positions on small islands at the far reaches of the Bombay archipelago, less out of concern for the fledgling English settlement on a neighboring island than as strategic vantages against one another, as well as the nearby Portuguese. However, tensions with the English soon began to emerge because Sidi Yakut insisted on harboring his fleet at Bombay during monsoon season. It was a request Company officials could not refuse, even though when the Sidi's men came ashore there were often altercations between them and the English soldiers and settlers. Some of these encounters ended in fatalities and political crises (Document 9).

The tensions got much worse after a change of policy within the English East India Company. By the early 1680s, the Company was facing a number of challenges, including growing threats from the Dutch and Portuguese, as well as what it perceived as increasing infringements on its rights from Mughal and other South Asian officials. The Company was also alarmed by a related problem—a dramatic rise in interloping, that is, English subjects trading with or traveling to the East Indies without Company license or permission. This in turn was related to growing political opposition to the Company at home, fueled both by a split in Company leadership and by the success of its opponents in linking it with the increasingly unpopular regimes of the late Stuart kings, Charles II and James II, and their Tory supporters.[10] Among the most controversial of these supporters was the London merchant and economic writer Josiah Child (1631–1699). During the 1680s, Child became the largest stockholder in the English East India Company. Because the amount of stock a person owned determined how many votes he could command, Child served at various points as the Company's governor, deputy governor, or just an extremely influential member of the Company's court of committees (board of directors). He and a small group of other men from the top echelon of Company stockholders also used their positions to great financial and political advantage, owning shares in ships leased to the Company, arranging low-cost sales of East India goods to themselves and their friends, and commanding outsized influence at court and with the Treasury and Royal Navy.

By the early 1680s, Child and his allies had become convinced that aggressive policies were needed to defend the Company's monopoly on trade in the East Indies. This meant engaging in a forward policy of lobbying at home, including instituting an annual "gift" to the monarch of more than £10,000. Yet Company leadership also saw this problem as partially rooted in politics in Asia. Interlopers could not succeed, they argued, without support from merchants and polities in India, particularly the Mughal Empire. Making matters worse, the Company faced growing challenges from its European rivals, particularly the Dutch who in 1682 had successfully supported a coup that resulted in the expulsion of the English factory from the Javanese port of Banten. There were also problems in the settlements themselves. In 1683, a garrison mutiny led by Captain Richard Keigwin lost the Company control of Bombay for upward of a year.

Child and others became convinced that only a show of force would arrest what they saw as the downward spiral of the Company. Beginning in the early 1680s, he and his circle encouraged a major program of shipbuilding in England aimed at developing a fleet of unusually large, heavily armed warships that could be used to police the interlopers, to overawe the Mughals, and to give the Dutch and Portuguese pause. The fleet would then also be available for other policing projects in and around the Indian Ocean. The Company also announced in 1687 that it was shifting its western Indian "Presidency" from Surat to Bombay, partly in order to gain more autonomy from the Mughals. Thus, its larger goal was not territorial expansion or empire in the modern sense but rather a defense of what it saw as its natural and negotiated rights in Asia: exclusive English trade and jurisdiction over all English subjects, especially favorable trading privileges; concessions on customs and other duties demanded by the Mughals; and the ability to defend itself against aggressors, especially other Europeans. It meant to send a signal to polities in Asia that the Company was to be taken seriously as both a political and a commercial power. There was also a more immediate objective. Company officials had come to believe that the rights and privileges they sought could not be secured permanently without a new, comprehensive farman from Emperor Aurangzeb, and they persuaded themselves that if this farman could not be obtained by diplomacy it would have to be won by war.

The prime agent of this policy in Asia was John Child (a close ally of but no relation to Josiah), the governor of Bombay and newly appointed general over all the Company's forces in Asia. From at least 1686 on, he was supported by that large fleet of English ships, all of them secretly authorized to seize not just the ships of English interlopers but also those of Mughal subjects (Document 10). The Company's war strategy was broad and involved four theaters of conflict: the Persian Gulf, to recover payments the English felt they were owed based on the agreement reached after the expulsion of the Portuguese in Hormuz in the 1620s; Siam, which had become a haven for English interlopers as well as a growing French ally; Bengal, where the Company also wanted expanded trading privileges as well as an independent settlement to fend off Mughal, Dutch, and Portuguese rivals alike; and, of course, western India, where the English felt military conflict would allow them to extract concessions from both the Mughals and the Portuguese.

As governor and general, John Child embraced the newly belligerent policy with enthusiasm mixed with some personal animosity, especially against the chief Mughal official in Surat, Mukhtiar Khan. As Child wrote in a letter back to London, "The Moors grow mighty insolent and it's high time they were taken down."[11] East India Company ships attempted to blockade Surat and began seizing ships up and down the coast—a policy many observers, both Mughal and European, saw as indistinguishable from piracy. At least twenty-one ships owned by Mughal subjects were captured and held, along with their goods. In some cases, the cargoes were judged as lawful "prize" (seizures) by Company Admiralty Courts (Document 4) and were either sold in India or sent back to England. The Company also took the opportunity to confiscate the ships and cargo of English interlopers. As a result of the Company's actions, trade in the region came almost to a standstill. Under great pressure from influential merchants at Surat who owned most of the captured ships, Mughal officials reacted swiftly, confiscating East India Company goods and monies, imprisoning their factors and other employees, and demanding not only that the Company return the seized goods but also that it return its trading headquarters to Surat.

The Portuguese and others made several attempts to broker a peace, but all of the attempts were resisted or bungled by one side or the other. John Child in particular apparently believed, like his mentors in London, that if he caused enough pain the Mughals would simply give in and grant the Company more favorable terms of trade. As a result, he gained a reputation with the Mughals and the Surat merchant elite for incivility, insolence, and irrational stubbornness. By the end of 1688, matters were at an impasse. Then Child made the fatal mistake, supposedly against the advice of more prudent subordinates, of seizing the provisioning fleet that was carrying grain to Sidi Yakut's army at Danda-Rajpuri. According to one source, Sidi Yakut asked several times for his ships to be returned and was rudely rebuffed (Document 13). It is possible that Sidi Yakut would never have been drawn into what amounted to a mercantile quarrel between Surat and Bombay had it not been for this incident. Or it may be that the Company's growing independence and assertiveness would have prompted action from the Mughals one way or the other. Either way, confrontation now became inevitable.

THE SIEGE OF BOMBAY

Sidi Yakut's forces disembarked at Sewri, a creek a few miles north of the main town of Bombay at about 2:00 a.m. on February 15, 1689. There is some disagreement about how many soldiers were involved, but 14,000 seems the most plausible number.[12] During the first few days after the invasion, the vastly outnumbered Company troops—approximately 300 European and Indo-Portuguese soldiers—were repeatedly forced back. The Sewri Fort was abandoned almost immediately, and outlying Company forts or fortlets, at Mahim, Mazagaon, and presumably Sion and Worli, were soon also evacuated. By February 17, the Sidi's forces were seen in the town itself "burning all before them," and within a few more days they had taken control of all the former territory of the Company except for Bombay Castle itself (usually referred to in James Hilton's diary as "the Fort"), a section of the town close to the fort, and a small area of perhaps no more than a square mile between the fort and the southern tip of Bombay Island (Mendham's Point). Sidi Yakut promptly set up his field headquarters at the Company's fort on Mazagaon Hill about two miles north of Bombay Castle.

During the next few days, the English hurriedly and belatedly prepared for a siege, slaughtering livestock, imposing rationing, and quartering the troops on Bombay Castle's various bastions. Governor Child also put in place the first of various defensive measures in case of a direct attack on the fort. For their part, the Sidi's forces established outposts and gun batteries in larger buildings in the town, notably the governor's own mansion, the East India House, and the "Portuguese" (Catholic) Church, three of the more imposing structures in Bombay. The Sidis also set up a battery on Dongri Hill, above and within easy shooting range of the fort.

Within weeks of the invasion, the governor and council had contracted with Sidi Yakut's great regional rivals, the Marathas, to supply reinforcements. The reinforcements began arriving on March 19, eventually comprising 2,000 men. Considerably smaller numbers of troops came from well-disposed Portuguese allies, though the Portuguese in many ways tried to play both sides of the conflict, some siding with the Sidi. The Maratha troops (referred to in Hilton's diary as "Savajees"), along with local Bhandari ("Bandareens"), Rajputs (north Indian soldiers), and Indo-Portuguese Catholics ("Topasses"), made up what Hilton calls the "black soldiers." These troops formed the backbone of the Company's defense.

Soon the Company's problems were compounded by epidemic disease, including an outbreak of the bubonic plague. On May 25, 1689, Governor Child ordered Hilton to "take a review or muster" of soldiers. The results of that suggest that an epidemic was already ravaging the forces and presumably the townspeople as well. By 1691, well over half of the settlement would die from disease. In addition, the defenders already had a serious desertion problem. Only two days after the invasion, on February 17, "most or all" (in Hilton's words) of the island's militia ran away to the mainland in boats. By the time of the March 25 muster, seventy more men, both European and Indo-Portuguese, had deserted, and it seems many of these took up arms for the Sidi. Later estimates were that sixty or more Europeans fought for the Sidi, and about half of these also converted to Islam. By the time the siege was lifted, at least 115 men had deserted, and only a handful of these are known to have returned.

By late March 1689, things had settled into a sort of routine. Sidi Yakut's army established entrenchments and batteries within and amid the ruined buildings of the by-now abandoned northern part of Bombay town and began constructing an elaborate network of trenches, tunnels, and earthworks that would, over the next year and a half, move closer and closer to the fort. In response, the Company's forces set up several of their own earthworks with batteries, built largely of palmare (palmyra or palm tree) boughs and earth. Every ten days to two weeks there was some sort of skirmish out in the open, usually between the Marathas and the Sidis, with European soldiers primarily used as backup. Both sides also attempted naval blockades of the other, and there were seizures of provision ships and exchanges of fire from ships as well as from batteries on shore. In addition, there were a number of miniature naval engagements, usually involving gallevats—large single- or double-masted rowboats, "war-boats with oars," armed with four to eight guns—and longboats from the European ships.

The hostilities abated only slightly during the monsoon months (roughly early June through early September), though some operations had to be aborted because of the violence of the rains. Around June, Company officials grew discouraged enough to actively seek a peace.

This would prove to be a long process. In the meantime, the fighting continued, more Maratha troops arrived, and the Sidis inched ever closer to the fort. Governor Child, who had instigated the conflict, now faded from the scene. Hilton mentions Child's being ill at the end of August 1689, with Child's last reported order coming on November 29, after which it appears that the fort was governed by Deputy Governor John Vauxe and the council,[13] which was itself being decimated by disease. Child died on February 4, 1690.

From November 1689 through March 1690, both sides focused on artillery exchanges, often at night. It is tempting to think that the relative decline in direct engagements reflected the impact of epidemic disease on both Sidi Yakut's and the Company's troop strength. In the meantime, Bombay had sent an embassy to negotiate terms, first with representatives from Surat at Portuguese Damão and then at the Mughal Court on campaign in the Deccan. (See Document 17.) On March 3, 1690, news finally reached Bombay that a definitive peace had been achieved, though it took more than a month longer to end the fighting — indeed, in the interim, the fighting grew more intense. Finally, on April 10, a messenger arrived from Surat to request that Sidi Yakut lift the siege.

During the next month and a half, James Hilton was involved in ferrying the peace articles back and forth between the fort and the Sidi camp; the peace documents presumably focused on logistical arrangements for getting Sidi Yakut's troops off the island. There was a prisoner exchange, and Hilton went with a free pardon to the Sidi camp for any Europeans who wanted to come back into the East India Company's employ. In the middle of all this, on May 28, came confirmation that William and Mary had been proclaimed king and queen back in England. Sidi Yakut began pulling out his troops on May 24, and the last of the troops left on June 22, blowing up Mazagaon Fort as a parting insult.

Sidi Yakut's forces never made a frontal attack on the fort, though there were many rumors that they would. Perhaps they were deterred by the determined defense, by the arrival of Maratha forces, or by the English artillery arrayed both on the fortress bastions and on the ships. It is also possible that the Sidi never intended to make a direct assault but instead sought to capitalize on the desertions, shortages of ordnance or food, and dwindling morale to force a surrender (Documents 14 and 15). Finally, the whole exercise may have had the aim of forcing the English to come to the bargaining table with the Surat merchants, which in the end was exactly what happened.

When the Sidi's forces finally departed, the infrastructure of Bombay lay in ruins. Larger buildings had been turned into gun batteries or reduced to rubble. Warehouses had been looted. Smaller houses had been pulled down or burned by one side or the other. More than one hundred people died directly as a result of fighting or bombardment, and many others likely died from their wounds. Well over a hundred more men deserted the garrison. Even more destructive of human life was epidemic disease, especially the plague, which almost certainly killed more people than the Sidi's army had. As Deputy Governor Vauxe would later write: "If this be the fruits of war, let them that love it have their bellies full; for I have had fate bad enough in it" (Document 19).

MAKING PEACE AND THE EMPEROR'S FARMAN

The concessions the Company had to make to get the siege lifted and receive its long-awaited farman proved extremely embarrassing. Despite a long list of demands of its own, the Company ultimately had to admit fault, compensate Surat merchants whose ships and goods it had seized, and make a large indemnity payment to the Mughal emperor, along with smaller payments to various officials. When the farman the Company had sought for so long finally arrived at Surat, it proved a major disappointment (Document 18). Its tone was offensive to Company officials' sensibilities, it offered no special privileges, and it demanded the banishment of John Child from India. This last condition, an overt challenge to Company sovereignty, was rendered moot by the fact that Child had already died. Nonetheless, it was a bitter blow, one that did not go unnoticed by the Company's critics and enemies.

What did the Mughals gain from this victory? The fact that there is little discussion of the English East India Company or of the siege in the official sources suggests that, while it loomed large for the English, it was not an issue of great moment to the Mughals. It seems probable that, from the Mughal point of view, the siege was a successful effort to knock an insufficiently deferential power down to size or it might simply have been seen as one incident among many in the Mughal–Maratha conflict, which consistently drew into its gravitational pull a range of local and regional powers. One must also remember that it was not the Mughal state itself but, as was typical, its tributary, Sidi Yakut Khan, who undertook the Bombay invasion. While the Mughals and the Sidis were closely allied, their aims with respect to the siege may not have been identical. Still, it would be a mistake to imagine that the English did not matter to the Mughals. Obviously, the Company's blockade and seizures of Mughal shipping out of Surat was seen as hostile—indeed a form of piracy — and it threatened the city's livelihood. Furthermore, some sources (see, for example, Document 24) suggest that Bombay's increasing attempts to assert its autonomy, even going so far as to coin its own money, were regarded by Mughal officials and perhaps even Aurangzeb himself as a challenge to their sovereign rights. One can almost see the invasion as the ultimate consequence of the Company's decision to move its trading headquarters from Surat to Bombay, a move that was extremely unpopular, not only because it seemed to be a hostile claim to power by the Company, but also because it represented a potentially significant loss of income for the political and merchant elite at Surat. This interpretation makes sense of one of the more puzzling features of the period after the siege — the fact that the Company was fairly quickly rehabilitated and ultimately received some trading concessions. And in fact the outcome might not have seemed so odd from the Mughal perspective. Once a rebellious noble was prepared to submit, he and his dependents were often reabsorbed into the Mughal governmental and military structure and sometimes even rewarded (Document 5). It was also clear that the world of trade in western India — and the revenues and customs it brought to places like Surat — had come to be fully integrated with the intra-Asian and Eurasian markets serviced by the European companies, and that Mughal officials, at least on the local level, did not treat that lightly.

It is also significant, though only clear in hindsight, that the period of the siege marked the high point of Mughal territorial expansion. Emperor Aurangzeb died at the age of eighty-eight in 1707, having spent close to three decades waging war in the Deccan and elsewhere at enormous cost in men and money. Overextended, and witnessing a rapid changeover of imperial leadership (there were six emperors in the dozen years after Aurangzeb's death), the empire began a rapid decentralization. Regional states within the empire, such as Bengal, now became essentially independent powers. While the empire lasted for another 150 years, it was soon reduced to a mainly titular power and, by the nineteenth century, to a largely symbolic entity under British domination. Meanwhile, the Marathas, who had been at one of their low points during the Siege of Bombay, recovered momentum in the eighteenth century and made major incursions into the former Mughal Empire. They would later be the premier power with which the East India Company had to contend, on land and at sea.

While the First Anglo-Mughal War and the siege in particular could hardly be said to have had a direct effect on the waning of Mughal power in the eighteenth century, it is well worth reflecting on its unforeseen long-term effects for English power in the region. Certainly, the Bengal phase of the war—which was always central to the Company's plans—had world-historical consequences. Though also apparently a military defeat that resulted at first in the retreat of Company forces, by the late 1690s the East India Company had acquired grants from both Aurangzeb and the nawab (provincial governor) of Bengal to build the town and fortification that became Calcutta, ultimately the capital of early British India. Meanwhile, the Siam and Persian Gulf conflicts contributed to the growing militarization of the Company's maritime fleet.

The Siege of Bombay had a somewhat different set of consequences. Relations both with Sidi Yakut and with the Mughals remained very tense for the rest of Aurangzeb's reign, and the Company was for some time deeply fearful of another invasion. Over the next several decades, the fort was rebuilt and strengthened with some sense of urgency, and other forts were built or refurbished across the archipelago. This was accompanied by a renewal of the Company's long-standing attempts to expand local jurisdiction at the expense of the Portuguese (especially the Portuguese Jesuits), bolstered now by the excuse that some Portuguese residents had either abandoned the Company in its hour of need or—it was alleged—offered material support to Sidi Yakut. At a longer remove, the impulse to greater command and control of both the land and the surrounding waterways led to the drainage of the tidewater causeways of the Bombay archipelago and their amalgamation into what became Greater Bombay. Ultimately this policy, coupled with determined maritime policing, undermined the power of all of the other competing coastal powers, including that of the Sidis, though it was not until the late eighteenth century that the latter were reduced to military insignificance. Through the first half of the eighteenth century, the Bombay council instituted policies designed to attract more settlers, rebuild both population and infrastructure, and engage in shipbuilding and other efforts that would ultimately lead to the creation of the Bombay Marine, a crucial aspect of eighteenth-century British domination over the Indian Ocean.

Indeed, naval power became, if anything, even more critical in the aftermath of the siege. The conflict had revolved around the seizure of ships and had blurred the lines for many between the East India Company and pirates. English critics jumped at the opportunity to delegitimize the Company's behavior; and some South Asian rivals used the moment to press the Company on its own promises to be opposing, rather than increasing, the "piratical threat" (Documents 23 and

24). In fact, the western Indian Ocean was becoming a more violent place. Piracy was a flexible and politicized category, and the decades between about 1690 and 1730 witnessed a dramatic rise in European maritime predation in the Indian Ocean, particularly from pirates coming from England and the Americas. At the same time, new maritime powers arose in the western Indian Ocean, such as the Qawasim from the northern coast of modern-day Oman (the so-called Muscat pirates) and revived Maratha power centers, particularly those associated with Kanhoji Angre (1669–1729), variously described as a "pirate" by the British and a "naval admiral" by the Marathas. The defeat of Kanhoji's successors helped by the 1750s to establish East India Company supremacy in the western Indian Ocean and ultimately even at Surat— at the same time that, after the Battle of Plassey of 1757, it began to acquire territorial power in Bengal to the east. Control of both land and sea were crucial to the subsequent expansion of the British Empire in India.

THE OUTCRY IN ENGLAND AND THE CAMPAIGN TO ABOLISH THE EAST INDIA COMPANY

If the consequences in Asia of the First Anglo-Mughal War, and especially the Siege of Bombay, are open to interpretation, there is little doubt that, from the Company's point of view, it had an outsized effect back in England. The East India Company had been a source of great controversy in English politics well before the war even began. Almost since its inception, the Company had been at the center of a debate over the best way to regulate trade and overseas expansion. Its leadership aggressively defended the Company's monopoly as the only effective way to manage not only trade but also diplomacy and war in so distant, alien, and "heathen" a place as Asia (Documents 4 and 20). Its rivals, by contrast, insisted that monopoly stifled commerce, artificially inflated consumer prices, and infringed on natural rights of trade and travel. The Company's policy of having the ships and goods of interlopers confiscated, in both Europe and Asia, and of prosecuting its enemies in court, created even more resentment and gave rise to a well-funded opposition that sought to have the Company either reformed under new leadership or abolished altogether (Document 21).

The coincidental timing of the First Anglo-Mughal War with the Revolution of 1688–89 only fueled these fires. The removal of James II as king in England and Scotland and the accession of William and Mary as joint rulers saw a revival of the political fortunes of the Whigs and the House of Commons. This posed major political and ideological problems for the Company, which had come to be associated for some with Toryism and royal absolutism. Enemies of the Company seized upon the war to argue that the Company had taken on the prerogatives of sovereignty—the power to wage war being one—that rightfully belonged to the monarch and that it was doing so illegitimately and incompetently, diminishing the reputation of England across the globe. Critics of the Company often set their sights on the person of Sir Josiah Child, who a decade earlier had helped to force a number of mostly Whig men of influence out of the Company. More unexpected constituencies also emerged, such as a group of East India Company sailors' wives and widows who petitioned the English Parliament in 1693 for redress against the Company (Document 22).

The widespread hostility toward the Company in the 1690s, coupled with the change of regime, gave rise to a sustained and highly organized effort to dissolve the Company and to establish a new one in its stead. It also gave rise to a notorious scandal, in which the Company was accused of paying large bribes to members of Parliament, including the speaker of the House of Commons, and to royal courtiers in order to hold on to its exclusive monopoly and quash efforts to create a new company. The Company's last-ditch efforts were to no avail, however. In 1698, William III and Parliament authorized the establishment of a rival company (known colloquially as the new East India Company), and for a time the two companies did political and financial battle both in Asia and in England. But this conflict would prove surprisingly short-lived: Both stockholders and politicians (often one and the same) quickly realized its futility and decided to merge the two companies into one. The United East India Company came into being in 1709, just two years after the union of England and Scotland created the modern state of Great Britain. Thus in the short term, the First Anglo-Mughal War helped fuel a near-mortal challenge to the East India Company. In the longer term, however, the crisis set the stage for a reinvigorated Company that was able to consolidate political and financial power in Britain as well as commercial and military power at sea and on land in Asia. Indeed, one could argue these early failures produced some of the preconditions—though hardly ones that contemporaries could have understood or anticipated—for the Company's ultimate military and administrative conquest of most of the South Asian subcontinent a century and some later.

JAMES HILTON AND HIS DIARY

Almost everything that is known about the day-to-day events of the siege comes from the diary of James Hilton (page 27), adjutant to Governor John Child, yet we know little about the man himself. He was sent from England in 1686 to serve as an ensign and, for some extra pay, adjutant (senior staff assistant in charge of organization and administration) in the Bombay garrison. He arrived in February 1687. At some point, he married the widow of another Company employee and they had a daughter named Mary. By the eve of the invasion, two years after he came to Bombay, he had been made captain, both of the militia and of the island's grenadier guard, by Governor John Child. Unlike his patron, Hilton survived the siege, though only barely. In 1691, he seems to have been recommended by the Bombay Council to head the first garrison company, and he was at that point the longest-serving officer in the garrison. It is not clear whether he took up the post, but if he did, he did not occupy it for very long. He died sometime in late December 1691 or early January 1692.

The diary itself is unsigned, but among other clues to its provenance is a letter accompanying the copy of the diary sent from Bombay to London after the end of the siege, which credits Hilton with its authorship. Still, it is evident from the text itself that Hilton was a soldier not a scholar. His spelling is erratic and phonetic (it has been regularized in this transcription), and the diary in the original uses almost no punctuation and tends to pile clause upon clause without clear beginnings or endings. In the seventeenth century, these were a common feature of texts penned by self-taught or lightly educated people; such people tended to write in the way they spoke.

Yet, if Hilton was not an accomplished prose writer, he was a seasoned raconteur. He is rather good at capturing the immediacy of armed conflict: its unpredictability, the inevitable problems of communication and supply, and the small acts of courage and teamwork (or their lack) that can spell victory or defeat. Good examples of this are the entries for February 15, 1689 (the day the Sidi's forces invaded), for March 10, 1690 (a bloody nighttime attack on one of the batteries), and for April 5, 1690 (an effort to undermine and blow up a second battery). And there are many others. Hilton also supplies valuable information about Mughal siege and battle tactics, particularly those of Sidi Yakut, whose presence looms large in the diary.

Still, the diary is hardly a disinterested account. This was not a "diary" in the sense we might imagine today: that is, a private journal.

Hilton was in a sense recording an official history of the siege, which both he and Governor John Child knew would be read with a critical eye by their superiors in London. So there is almost nothing in the diary that could be construed as critical either of the East India Company or of John Child, and a good deal that, in retrospect, was probably white-washing. In fact, the diary almost always puts the most positive possible gloss on the actions of the defenders. A striking example of this is the account of the rout of Lieutenant Paul Paine's forces at the beginning of the diary, during which Ensign Alexander Monroe and more than a dozen others were killed. It is instructive to compare Hilton's description of these events, and many others, with the highly critical account of the same episode that appears in Alexander Hamilton's discussion of the conduct of the war (Document 13). At the same time, while Hilton does not or cannot express his views explicitly (and, in fact, we have little way of knowing what he really thought), his is a vivid record, perhaps inadvertently, of the challenges facing the fort during the siege, especially among the soldiery, whose low morale, desertions, and mutinies are leitmotifs of Hilton's account.

As is true of many accounts from the field, Hilton's statistical reportage should be viewed with some skepticism. He almost certainly over-estimates the size of the Sidi's forces, and he is also quite optimistic—at times fanciful—about the amount of damage inflicted on the enemy by the English and their allies. There are also problems with the casualty figures for his own side, made worse by the persistent ethnic chauvinism that pervades the account. Despite this, Hilton's diary is rich with detail on the daily lives of these soldiers and sailors attempting to withstand the stress, food shortages, sickness, and claustrophobia of a sixteen-month siege. Moreover, though civilians are clearly not among Hilton's main concerns, we get a sense of their conditions during the siege, not only in the grim reports of deaths but also in the numerous glimpses of the lives of townspeople, including women, children, laborers, servants, and others we might think of as "non-combatants."

CONCLUSION

The English at Bombay were venturing rather late into a world of great complexity. There was an abundance of powerful and already established political and politico-commercial polities on the Indian subcontinent: the dwindling yet still intimidating coastal empire of the Portuguese Estado da India; the seemingly ever-rising power of the Dutch East India Company; the centuries-old and still expanding Mughal

Empire; the relatively new but increasingly formidable Maratha Empire; and many others. Though deeply connected in many ways to the world of Atlantic colonization—from the silver that fueled commercial expansion to the many Euro-American pirates who helped destabilize the late seventeenth- and eighteenth-century Indian Ocean—this was also a very different environment from the Americas. While Europeans could leverage their power at sea to dominate over scattered littoral regions and some smaller coastal polities, even the Dutch and the Portuguese—let alone the English, French, and Danes—could hardly pretend to have martial, commercial, or political superiority in Asia, especially with respect to large and well-established territorial empires. Moreover, Asian populations did not suffer catastrophic death from the encounter with foreign microbes in the way that the indigenous peoples of the New World did; indeed, to the contrary, European mortality from disease was one of the greatest challenges to settlement and colonization efforts in Asia—as Bombay demonstrated. Although it can be plausibly argued that European trade and colonization created an "Atlantic world," this was clearly not the case in the Indian Ocean, which was being crisscrossed by people, ships, and merchandise for millennia before any European hoisted his sail there.

In the seventeenth century, the English East India Company sought to set itself up as both a commercial and a sovereign power, but its position was extremely ambiguous and tenuous. Its legitimacy as a trading monopoly, as well as its right to deploy force, derived from the English king, but its continued presence on the South Asian subcontinent—as the Siege of Bombay clearly showed—depended on the sufferance of the Mughal emperor. The Company needed both English charters and Mughal farmans to support its ambitions. However, the Company was also willfully independent, establishing armed and fortified settlements, law courts, and diplomatic regimes that, while small in size and confined to the coasts, nevertheless sought to operate autonomously. The Company thus represented the complexity and pluralism of sovereignty so evident across early modern Eurasia. Meanwhile, Bombay itself was a sort of microcosm of an imperial crossroads. Nominally under English sovereignty, the lines between the English crown and Company remained blurred, while a host of powers—Portuguese, Mughal, Maratha, Sidi, and Dutch, as well as different coalitions of settlers on the islands—contended for position and jurisdiction at various points around and within the archipelago.

Thus, though the Siege of Bombay and the First Anglo-Mughal War were in some sense passing moments in the greater history of the Indian Ocean, they tell us a great deal about the early modern Eurasian world and the prehistory of modern European empire in Asia. The English did not arrive dominant over a subservient indigenous population, nor were the seventeenth-century Europeans in Asia under the thumb of local powers. Rather, both coexisted and overlapped in a complex of negotiated relationships that involved ever-shifting regimes of both alliance and violence. Greatly complicating this picture was the intricate racial, ethnic, and religious makeup of South Asia, which, in itself, played a major role in creating the contingent world in which both Asians and Europeans sought to operate. Mughal Surat depended heavily on trade and navigation, not only of merchants from the wider Asian world but also of Europeans, and Surat's leaders clearly fought quite hard to retain these people under their authority at the same time that they deeply distrusted them. Conversely, who would have predicted that the English East India Company, a number of whose directors, including Josiah Child, were also deeply involved in the expanding Atlantic slave trade, would find its flagship settlement brought to its knees by a military commander who was ethnically African and, according to some sources, a former slave? While a single incident in a much larger story, the Siege of Bombay focuses our minds on just how little people know of their own future and, conversely, how careful students of history need to be about projecting the assumptions of their contemporary world into the past. It also shows that even in the seventeenth century, local events had global reverberations and vice versa. Indeed, the accelerated cultural and geographical convergences across the early modern world led to new and unpredictable encounters, unusual institutional arrangements, and personal and collective challenges whose character we in the twenty-first century are still trying to understand.

NOTES

[1] Sidi Yakut Khan's given name was Sidi Qasim; the English in this period often referred to him simply as "the Sidi" (often spelled "Siddy"). In this collection, he is referred to as Sidi Yakut, Sidi Yakut Khan, or the Sidi.

[2] The distinction between the two is important and often misunderstood. A "factory" was a trading outpost, located within a port or trading town under another jurisdiction, which usually consisted of a residence for the Company's "factors" (i.e., trade representatives), warehouses, and other buildings necessary for trade. A "settlement" was a place the English East India Company actually governed, such as Madras (or Fort St. George, known today as Chennai) on the east coast of India and Bombay (known today as Mumbai) just off the west coast.

[3] Two influential discussions of the problem of contingency are Kenneth Pomeranz, *The Great Divergence: China, Europe, and the Making of the Modern World Economy* (Princeton, N.J.: Princeton University Press, 2000), and Lauren Benton, *Law and Colonial Cultures: Legal Regimes in World History, 1400–1900* (Cambridge: Cambridge University Press, 2002).

[4]Alison Games, *The Web of Empire: English Cosmopolitans in an Age of Expansion, 1560–1660* (New York: Oxford University Press, 2008), 14.

[5]Sanjay Subrahmanyam, "Connected Histories: Notes towards a Reconfiguration of Early Modern Eurasia," *Modern Asian Studies* 31, no. 3 (1997): 735–62; Sanjay Subrahmanyam, *Explorations in Connected History: From the Tagus to the Ganges* (Delhi: Oxford University Press, 2004).

[6]"Mughal" (or "Mogol") is a Perso-Arabic corruption of "Mongol."

[7]Verenigde Oost-Indische Compagnie in Dutch.

[8]While technically Sivaji was crowned Chhatrapati (king or emperor) in 1674, he had begun consolidating power considerably earlier, from the late 1650s on.

[9]A mansab was an appointment and a rating of a Mughal noble, who would then be referred to as a mansabdar, or rank-holder. Mughal nobles were rated by the number of cavalry and horses they could theoretically raise for battle, though increasingly the mansabdari system was more a scheme of accounting than an actual census of troop readiness and availability. Often, mansabdars were incentivized and rewarded for their service by jagirs, or grants of revenue over lands, though frequently not lands under their own control and influence.

[10]In the late 1670s and 1680s, the "Tory" political faction supported the right of James, Duke of York, a Roman Catholic, to succeed his brother as King James II. The "Whig" faction, by contrast, favored finding an alternative, Protestant candidate for the throne.

[11]Surat to London, April 26, 1684, British Library, IOR E/3/44 fol. 43.

[12]Fourteen thousand is the number that Sidi Yakut himself gave at the height of the siege. Other estimates ranged from 6,000 to 30,000.

[13]The governing council consisted of the top Company officials on the island and usually any fleet captains who happened temporarily to be in port.

PART TWO

The Siege of Bombay: A Soldier's Diary

JAMES HILTON

Diary of the Siege of Bombay
February 15, 1689, to June 22, 1690

February 15, 1689

On Friday 15th February in the morning about 2 o-clock the Sidi landed at Sewri[1] with 125 boats of men, ammunition, provision and all things fit for war computed to be about six thousand men. The Corporal that was posted there on the landing fired and gave the alarm to Mazagaon[2] which soon alarmed the Fort at Bombay by the firing there. Immediately the General came out and ordered the alarm gun to be fired and came down and opened the gates. In the meanwhile Lieutenant Nangle, who was quartered at the East India House, marched out with Captain Clifton's company as far as his advance guard which was at the Seven Brabs.[3] In the meanwhile the General ordered out Mr. Utworth and Sergeant Jones on horseback to see where the Enemy was, who brought word that the Enemy was approaching towards Mazagaon and that Lieutenant Nangle was engaged on them between Mazagaon and Sewri. The General asked them what number of men the Enemy might consist of, who answered about three or four hundred, the same he told Lieutenant Nangle, which made him advance the readier to beat the Enemy off the Island. But when [Lieutenant Nangle] came nigh them to engage [i.e., to fight] instead of three or four hundred [he] found there a body of our Enemy consisting of about six thousand men. About 4 o-clock in the morning the General [Sir John Child] ordered me with his Guard of Grenadiers[4] to go and discover about the town, but [we] saw none of the Enemy. The General, ordering the manchua[5] to be ready, took fifteen of

---

[1] Sewri was a village on Bombay's eastern coast, about four or five miles north of the Fort.

[2] Mazagaon was one of the islands of the Bombay archepelago. The Company maintained a small fort there.

[3] A variety of palm tree, common at Bombay; the "Seven Brabs" refers to an area south of Mazagaon.

[4] The general's personal guard.

[5] A single-masted cargo boat.

"Bombay Diary" [1689]–90. British Library, India Office Records G/3/3 (3).

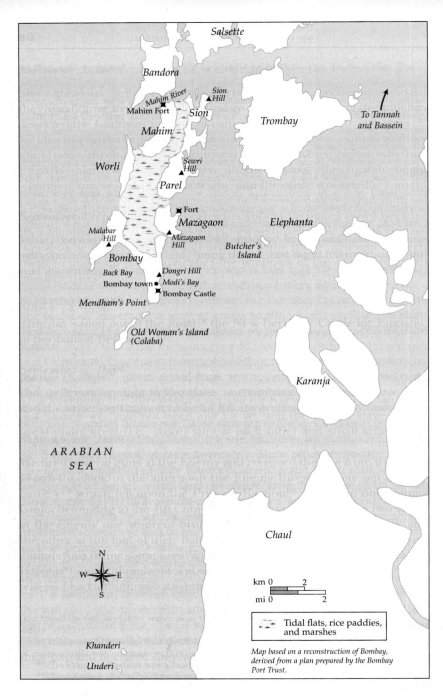

Map 2. *Bombay, 1680s*

the grenadiers and ordered them on board her under the command of Ensign Browne to go and annoy the Enemy what they could.

In the meanwhile orders was given to get the horses ready and pistols laden and one of our horse scouts came in and told the General that Lieutenant Nangle was hotly engaged and wanted ammunition, upon which it was immediately ordered with a corporal and four files[6] of musketeers. Captain Clifton, Mr. Edward Cornwall, Mr. Henry Thurscross, and Mr. Nicolas D'Mello were ordered out with horses to see where the Enemy lay, who riding up on a hill beyond Mazagaon, espied a vast number of the Enemy not less than [blank space in manuscript] men and Lieutenant Nangle engaged [illegible] . . . at the foot of the hill. When [i.e., Then] Mr. Edward Cornwall rode down to him and told him his safest way (if possible) was to retreat to the Fort at Bombay, that at Mazagaon being but a place of small strength. But his [Lieutenant Nangle's] men being all so tired by so far marching and engaging could not hold out therefore concluded to go to Mazagaon Fort and use their utmost there. On which Captain Clifton and horsemen made their way to Bombay and acquainted the General what they had seen and that Lieutenant Nangle with most of his men were near Mazagaon Fort when [they] left him, on which the General ordered Lieutenant Paul Paine out with Captain Vauxe his Company to the relief of Lieutenant Nangle who by that time he had gone to the foot of the hill of Mazagaon. There the Enemy came running down upon him and [they] engaged one another but being overpowered by the Enemy's number [and] making his retreat [Lt. Paine] lost his Ensign, Mr. Alexander Monroe and fourteen men and the party that was carrying Lieutenant Nangle's provision [was] all cut off.

At the same time that Lieutenant Paine was ordered out the General ordered out his own Company commanded out by Ensign Osboldiston (Captain Gowen Ansley being then on the Guard) out to be a reserve to Lieutenant Paine and to lodge himself in the batty ground [i.e., rice paddy] beyond the Portuguese [Catholic] Church. But he hearing Lieutenant Paine and Enemy engaged marched towards Mazagaon to his succor [i.e., to aid him] and found them in great disorder, the Enemy pressing upon him in multitudes. But upon his [Ensign Osboldiston's] arrival the Enemy stood [i.e., paused and did not advance] which gave Lieutenant Paine time to rally his men and put them into order so that both then engaged the Enemy and killed them a great many men. When [i.e., Then] the Enemy retreated to the top of Mazagaon Hill where they

---

[6] A detachment of troops.

joined with the rest of the army that came in multitudes from their boats at Sewri, and Lieutenant Paine and Ensign Osboldiston on that retreated back to the Fort.

Ensign Browne being come back gave the General an account of the Enemy's number of boats and that they were all dry ashore at Sewri. And the General having ordered the European commanders before to send their boats ashore manned and ordered the manchua with them to go and use their utmost to burn and destroy the Enemy's boats having ordered combustible stuff for the same. And if that Lieutenant Nangle (not knowing but that he might be cut off) were in Mazagaon to give him what aid and assistance they could possibly give. When they got up to Sewri they found the Enemy's boats so far hauled up under the hill where the Enemy had planted a battery of cannon up on the hill to secure them their boats that they could not be come at and [the Enemy] galled [i.e., harassed] them so with their great and small shot that it was impossible to effect what they designed. So they came to Mazagaon under the fort there [and] finding them and the Enemy engaged called out to know if Lieutenant Nangle was there. When [i.e., to which] it was answered yes and that they wanted ammunition, upon which they ordered in a small boat with what ammunition they could spare.

The Enemy then coming down and firing thick at the boats they were forced to haul off, in which time Lieutenant Nangle wrote a note to the General giving an account of his condition, which note he sent per [i.e., by] an Englishman which swam off with it in his mouth to the manchua, the Enemy shooting several [bullets] around at him, some of which he took out of the water and brought along with the note and delivered [to] the General, on the receipt of which the General immediately ordered two great guns to be sent to Lieutenant Nangle at Mazagaon with ammunition suitable to what [he] wrote for.

About 11 o-clock in the morning the General ordered me with twenty-three files of men to the Sessions House to secure the town and about 4 o-clock in the afternoon [we] should march to the Portuguese Church, sending me two field pieces with ammunition, and ordered the Militia and Bandareens[7] under the command of one William James to go as far as the Seven Brabs and continue there until further order, and if overpowered by the Enemy to retreat to the Portuguese Church. We passed that night pretty quietly: a small skirmish or two we had at the Portu-

---

[7] Bandareens (bhandari) were a Hindu caste in maritime western India, often engaged in military or agrarian service.

guese Church and one they had at the Seven Brabs, but beat the Enemy off [with?] one Bandareen and three soldiers.

February 16, 1689

In the morning we heard great firing at Mazagaon, the General having ordered the boats to endeavor a second attempt on the Enemy's vessels. The Militia engaged with [a] great part of the Enemy's army and sent to the Portuguese Church for some assistance, upon which Ensign Osboldiston was sent with eight files of men and there fought the Enemy in the batty ground for above an hour. And then Sergeant FitzGerald with four files of men more was ordered out to engage with a party of the Enemy that came between our party and the Church, which gave opportunity to Ensign Osboldiston and the militia to retreat to the Church. And then the Enemy took the woods and Dongri[8] to surround the Church, on consideration of which, and the Fort being weak having but a few people, Ensign Osboldiston and I with our men withdrew to the Fort and the Enemy retreated to Mazagaon Hill with a considerable loss of men.

And by 6 o-clock this morning here arrived Senhor [i.e., Sir] Christopher D'Soaza with a letter from Lieutenant Nangle to the General that gave an account of three batteries that the Enemy had raised and that it was impossible to hinder them [they] being so numerous. Upon which the General about 4 o-clock in the afternoon ordered Lieutenant Nangle to quit Mazagaon Fort with his men in boats ordered upon purpose. The boats that were sent on the second attempt of destroying the Enemy's boats being returned, [they] gave the General an account of their hot service and how they destroyed two of the Enemy's boats by setting them on fire, one of which blew up being full of powder and [the like].

Since the beginning of our first service the General has been without [i.e., outside] the gate giving out of orders and the President setting at the gateway ordering ammunition and powder as the people came in for it. That night his Excellency ordered the call be beat[9] about 6 o-clock and ordered eight files of men under the command of Captain Clifton to lie out beyond Doctor Bird's [house] all night and keep good looking out for the Enemy's approaching. And [we] passed the night indifferently quiet, only there was some small alarms.

---

[8] In the original, "Dungaree": a hill and fort just to the north of Bombay Castle.
[9] A drumbeat used to give notice to soldiers to gather, often for return to quarters, mustering, or on occasion of an alarm.

February 17, 1689

This morning our Guard from the East India House gave us an account of a great many of the Enemy marching down towards the town. The General ordered out a party of eight files of men under the command of Lieutenant Paine to go to the house by John Deare's where we used to dry the powder and where was used to make powder. And if in case he found any powder there to blow it up or to throw it into a tank and to set on fire those cadjan[10] houses that were about the town beyond the Portuguese Church, for the General was informed that they [the enemy] used to shelter themselves there. And from thence to march to Dongri and set all those houses afire that was beyond the East India House, which was accordingly performed.

This day we had most or all of our Militia run away to the other side in boats and about 10 o-clock this morning Lieutenant Nangle and Ensign Osboldiston with two or three horsemen more went and scoured about the town up as high as John Deare's and so unto the bay, where they met with a party of the Enemy under a tree beyond the Portuguese Church, but the Enemy retreated and have no way annoyed us this night. This morning Captain James Hilton[11] with two more horsemen rode to the Portuguese Church and so down the bay, but espied none of the Enemy and about 8 o-clock this morning the East India House guard withdrew and gave us an account of the Enemy's being in town, upon which the General ordered Ensign Osboldiston with a party of men to go and fight them and Captain Gowen Ansley with another strong party of men to be his reserve. The Enemy was very numerous and came on very thick upon them but he and Captain Ansley both engaged them in the town (where the Enemy burnt all before them) for at least five hours. The General himself being out at that time at the end of the bazaar with Captain Cooke and several others and sent his grenadiers that he had with him for their assistance, he having but a few men then in the Fort. The Enemy visibly lost a considerable number of men, our loss not above four or six men, and Lieutenant Nangle with that party of Captain Clifton's Company that were off of duty [were ordered] to go out and relieve Captain Ansley and Ensign Osboldiston. In this time Captain Gary [was] coming from the Sidi with a message of a cessation of arms [i.e., a cease-

---

[10] Small huts thatched with coconut or palm tree leaves where poorer people lived.
[11] The author here peculiarly refers to himself in the third person (unlike elsewhere in the manuscript). This suggests the possibility that he was not the only author of this document.

fire]; at night Lieutenant Nangle being commanded in, Captain Vauxe went out with a party to lie out all night.

February 19, 1689

The General ordered Ensign Carney, Commander of the Fort at Mahim,[12] to spoil and demolish the Fort at Mahim and so to repair [i.e., proceed] to Bombay.

February 20, 1689

His Excellency gave out orders in the evening and having before given orders to Mr. Cooke, Mr. Weldon, Mr. Edwards and Mr. Hibbins, and Mr. Stanley to be Commissaries of the Provision ordered every Company to go daily to them and receive their allowances of rice, dal and butter, and likewise ordered men to go and drive out what cattle could be got and ordered Mr. Walton's man, the butcher, to kill them, ordering for his assistance eight men out of every Company in order to the salting thereof, and that those pieces that would not take salt as the heads and [such-like] bloody pieces to be delivered out to the several Companies as they were quartered on the several bastions, and also ordered the out-guards to be kept at the bunder[13] and [such-like] places.

February 22, 1689

This afternoon the General gave out an order that all the halberds[14] and half-pikes[15] should be brought upon the bastions and curtains to be dispersed about for the defense of the Fort. Ever since we have had Captain Gary pass to and from the Sidi and have been about treating of peace seemingly, and one Nur Mahmud, an old servant of the Sidi's, has been sent often to us with messages about peace but only to delay time. And [we] have been alarmed after every night and houses set on

---

[12] Mahim was the northwesternmost island and village of the Bombay archipelago. By vacating the Mahim Fort, the authorities in Bombay were ceding control of most of Bombay to the Sidi.

[13] The word probably comes from the Persian *bandar*, meaning warehouse, pier, or port. In this case, Hilton is referring to the Company's quay and warehouses off Bombay town.

[14] An infantry weapon, consisting of an axe blade and spear, mounted on a long (5–7 ft.) handle.

[15] An infantry weapon, also known as a spontoon, of about six or seven feet—as the name implies, it is about half the size of a normal pike.

fire notwithstanding their pretensions of treaty which is only to weary and tire us.

February 23, 1689

Captain Barber arrived here from Persia.[16]

March 15, 1689

His Excellency last night about 11 o-clock sent for me and ordered me to give orders for the soldiery to go to sleep, for by break of day he designed to engage the Enemy, the which accordingly was performed.

March 16, 1689

About 6 o-clock this morning the manchua, Ensign John Browne, Commander, began to fire and upon her firing the rest of the frigates (being the Emerald and the Ruby) that were appointed to batter down the battery that was raised at Dongri Hill and the [frigates] Nessamy and Hunter were ordered to be manned out of the Europe ships, which plied their shot very hotly at the Enemy's battery and so did we from the Fort, but discerning them to fire guns from his Honor's house[17] at our shipping, his Excellency ordered some guns to be plied at the said house as well as at their battery and [the] Portuguese Church where we knew they had an entrenchment. The sea commanders came ashore with their boats' crews and eased our soldiers in plying the cannon and soon brought down his Honor's house. And his Honor Mr. Mitchell[18] being on the Plum Tree Bastion[19] ordered some guns to ply at the battery as well as at the Portuguese Church, which shot visibly did great execution. His Excellency ordered two Shiraz[20] bottles of wine to every Company and so likewise proportionately to the sailors for drams.

His Excellency had advice by the Bandareens that there was a great part of the Enemy in the woods upon which he ordered Lieutenant Nangle to have eight files of men out of the Garrison to join with that party of Lieutenant Paul Paine commanded out last night, and that of

---

[16] East India Company ships frequently sailed up the Indian coast and into the Persian Gulf to trade with the Persian (Safavid) Empire, where the Company also maintained factories.

[17] Both sides set up batteries inside buildings or the ruins of buildings.

[18] Thomas Mitchell, president at Bombay and second of the Bombay council.

[19] One of the landward-facing bastions of Bombay Fort.

[20] Shirazi wine was a famous white wine produced in the area of Shiraz, Persia, not to be confused with the French Shiraz or Syrah grape and wine.

the Bandareen guard which was four files commanded by Sergeant FitzGerald, and the Militia and Bandareens (the number being very few for that of the Militia not consisting of above twenty). And his Excellency ordered two files of his own Guard to go with him to attack the Enemy where he was informed they lay. And coming up through the woods, the said Lieutenant Nangle commanding Ensign Osboldiston to take that part of the woods that went up by Captain Beere's [house], and Lieutenant Paine to take the lower way of the same woods. And in case they met with the Enemy to beat an alarm (each of them having a drum with them) and then he would march up to their assistance with a main body. But finding none of the Enemy [they] marched straight through the woods and at a house the advanced party, being two files of grenadiers, marched up to their walls and fired at the Enemy. And Lieutenant Nangle coming up they [the Enemy] all run away, returning down a little below the Portuguese Church so he marched back to the Fort. His Excellency in the meantime ordered that none of the cannon should be plied towards the town but altogether to ply at their [the Enemy's] battery at Dongri Hill at which we placed a great many shot and believe disabled some of their guns.

In this morning's service was placed three shot into his Excellency's lodging and one shot took off a man's arm on the Flagstaff Bastion,[21] the shipping continuing all the time plying their shot as also the manchua. What damage they have received we refer it to tomorrow's account having no certain news what damage they received, only Ensign Browne supposed to be killed. Upon [the hearing of] which his Excellency ordered that if it was so that Mr. William Utworth should command the manchua and follow such orders [as] he should give him. Captain Andrews being all the day on the Tank Bastion and Captain James Cooke up on the Plum Tree Bastion[22] plied them guns which did great execution. And at night the General ordered all the guns upon the curtain to be laden with partridge[23] for fear of their approaching nigher.

March 17, 1689

About 2 o-clock this morning the General had news brought him of a party of the Enemy being at Captain Oglethorpe's house, but when he

---

[21] One of the seaward bastions of Bombay Fort.

[22] The Tank and Plum Tree Bastions were the two landward bastions of the Fort.

[23] That is, to load the guns with small shot (shot suitable for shooting fowl). The intent was to have the shot spray out widely to deter or discourage anyone who sought to attack the Fort under cover of darkness.

sent out to see found it to be a false report of the Bandareens. About 5 o-clock this morning his Excellency went round the works[24] and ordered the guns to be fired upon the battery. And notwithstanding that we had, as we thought, quite disabled his Honor's house the day before, they again fired afresh from thence. So [his Excellency] ordered them to ply their guns there as well as at the Portuguese Church and their battery at Dongri Hill. And about 6 o-clock this morning the several commanders aforementioned came ashore with their men and took the said several posts and in about half an hour disabled them [the Enemy] from firing at [i.e., from] his Honor's house and so continued firing round the Fort all day, which we believe did the Enemy great damage. About 11 o-clock Dr. Mitchell came ashore from the hospital ship and brought this following account of our men that were killed and wounded in this service hitherto:

[The list, redacted here for space, was signed by Robert Mitchell, Chirurgeon (i.e., surgeon), and states that nine Englishmen and seven "Portuguese" were either dead or "dangerous" (seriously wounded)].

We had this day but one man killed who was one Scales, a grenadier. A shot from their battery took him sponging a gun upon the Low Bastion.[25] The Enemy threw some few rockets which did us no damage at all. At night the General ordered the guns to be laden with partridge and grape shot for fear of their [the Enemy's] nigher approach. And about 10 o-clock at night, having news brought him from a Bandareen that was sent per his Excellency who passed the out-guards and went up as high as his Honor's house, but they would let him go no further, so [he] returned back with news that they [the Enemy] were hard at work at his Honor's house, so his Excellency ordered some guns to be fired at them and have expended in powder about 110 barrels. Also have received a great many shot from the Enemy, but thank God have done us no more hurt than what is here mentioned.

March 18, 1689

The shot that we fired yesterday about 2 o-clock we are informed did great execution. Sidi Qasim [i.e., Sidi Yakut] himself being at that time walking down to direct and see their works, one of our shot grazed just by him and beat the dirt up in his face which occasioned their leaving off

---

[24] The various defensive structures, earthworks, and so on.
[25] Swabbing the bore of a gun between firings.

work at that time. His Excellency this morning by break of day ordered the guns to be fired, the Enemy first firing at our battery ships. About 6 o-clock the said several commanders came ashore with their boats' crews and took their usual posts and plied the Enemy's battery, his Honor's house and the Portuguese Church very hotly. We had one man killed which was of Captain Cooke's boat's crew as he was priming a gun on the Plum Tree Bastion.

His Excellency was informed by a letter he received from Captain Gary that on Saturday last being [the] 16th instant[26] we had killed the Enemy that day twelve men and a shot came and split one of their guns and we believe we have done them a great deal more mischief these last two days. On board the battery ship we had one man killed outright belonging to the Shrewsbury, one soldier's leg shot off and a seaman and a soldier wounded. [At] about 10 o-clock at night and about 1 o-clock and 3 [o-clock] again his Excellency ordered the guns to be fired, but received none from the Enemy.

March 19, 1689

The [ship] Caesar, Captain Wright, from China arrived here. His Honor Mr. Mitchell was this day taken very ill and likewise Captain Consett. This morning his Excellency ordered the guns to be fired at their battery but received none from the Enemy again but all was very quiet. About 7 o-clock this morning there came fifteen gallevats[27] from Ram Rajah[28] and when they came nigh the shore his Excellency ordered that they should not land until such time [as] we were satisfied who they were. And afterwards the chiefs of them were conducted up to his Excellency by Captain Richard Clifton and myself. We received but very few shot from the Enemy all this day until about 4 or 5 o-clock at night, when they began to fire and so continued until it was dark. And the General ordered the guns to be placed ready to be fired at them in the night which was accordingly performed.

March 20, 1689

The Charles and John, Captain Wale Commander, from the Coast arrived here. This morning we fired at the Enemy who was indifferent

---

[26] That same month [that is, March 16].

[27] Large single- or double-masted rowboat, armed with four to eight guns and very common on the Malabar Coast. The gallevat was often used for transporting soldiers.

[28] Rajaram Bhonsle (r. 1689–1700) succeeded his half-brother Sambhaji as Maratha emperor.

quiet until about 7 o-clock. Our Bandareens and Savajees[29] went to engage the Enemy at the Brahmanys' house,[30] where they heard there was a party of them and when they came they found about 200 of the Enemy there which they soon put to flight and pursued them within musket shot of the Portuguese Church, where there sallied out upon the Bandareens above one thousand of the Enemy, and being over-numbered by them [they] were forced to retreat with the loss of one man and another wounded. But our men say they killed several of the Enemy, one whereof, Daud by name, well known by the Bandareens being an Inhabitant of the Island, was killed. We from the Fort continued firing at the Enemy's battery and they returning again. On board our battery ships we had three men wounded and one on shore being a Savajee. A shot took off his leg as he was sitting in the house of Mr. Pindar. This day there ran away from the 2d Company Anton D'Soaza and William Church. At night his Excellency ordered the Issabux[31] to fall down and lie against their battery. Also his Excellency being upon the bastion about 11 o-clock at night ordered the guns to be fired and also again at 1 o-clock.

March 21, 1689

This morning the General ordered the guns to be fired and the Enemy fired at us again. The Commanders coming ashore and taking their aforesaid posts we continued firing at the Enemy's batteries and the Portuguese Church. There was one man killed today on the Tank Bastion (being Richard Finch of the 3d Company) who, standing close by his Excellency, was taken on the head with a shot. Also this day the Arab ship that had lain here some time sailed from the Fort towards Muscat.[32] In the evening we had brisk firing on both sides. Captain Cooke went on board [the] 18th instant and has hitherto continued very ill. His Excellency ordered the guns to be fired about 9 o-clock at night and about 11. Also the spies sent out by our Bandareens brought word that the Enemy was hard at work at the Brahmanys' house and his Excellency ordered them to go out and engage them, but they returned and

---

[29] Maratha soldiers. This idiomatic term derives from Sivaji or Shivaji Bhonsle, the progenitor of the Maratha Empire, who died in 1680.

[30] The Brahmanys' house was presumably a house belonging to a prominent Brahmin.

[31] The Issabux was a Surat ship that had been seized as prize by the Company in mid-1687. This somewhat obscure passage probably refers to the crew manning the prize, who were apparently assisting with shore defense.

[32] The Arabian port, now the capital of Oman.

found not the Enemy, so his Excellency about 1 o-clock ordered the guns to be fired again.

March 22, 1689

This morning the General ordered the Bandareens to go and scout out as usual but saw none of the Enemy (except a few at Captain Gary's house) who as soon as they saw our Bandareens they ran away. This morning also Dr. Robert Mitchell came from on board the hospital ship and brought this following account:

18th instant: that one William Saunders was mortally wounded and dead.

20th [instant]: Christopher Willcox dangerously wounded.

[Signed], John FitzGerald, Sergeant.

About 11 o-clock in the morning the Bandareens brought in three of the Enemy supposed to be spies and presently after we heard our Bandareens engaging the Enemy in the Company garden. The Enemy overpowering them in number his Excellency ordered out sixteen files from the Garrison to their assistance who engaged them also. But our firing three or four great guns amongst them made them soon retreat. We continued firing from the Fort all the day and they at us again from their battery at night. His Excellency ordered the guns for their firing in the night time, which was accordingly performed. One of the Savajee commanders that brought over the first party was killed in the engagement above mentioned and another wounded.

March 23, 1689

This morning the guns were fired per his Excellency's order and the Enemy fired out of their new battery at the East India House as well as at their old battery at his Honor's house and Dongri Hill, who fired very hotly at our battery ship and killed only my little boy Samuel.[33]

The General ordered the town to be burnt which was accordingly performed by the Bandareens. We continued firing at their battery all the day and so did our battery ships and at night his Excellency as was usual ordered the guns to be placed in order to their being fired in the night, which was performed. Also this day one Diego Creade run away from the 4th Company. This evening after his Excellency had given Ram

---

[33] "My little boy Samuel" may have been a servant or slave, since he is never given a last name.

Rajah['s] subadar[34] that brought over the men a good gratuity he went away with seven of his gallevats to his master to get a good supply of more men.

March 24, 1689

This morning early his Excellency ordered the guns to be played upon the [Enemy] batteries which was accordingly done, and about 9 o-clock sent for me and ordered me to let the soldiery have two bottles of Shiraz wine to each Company and one to the gunners which I saw performed. Lieutenant Edwards being very ill these four or five days [he] went on board the hospital ship. Today we kept firing at the Enemy all day and at night the General ordered the guns to be placed as usual.

March 25, 1689

This morning his Excellency ordered me to take a review or muster of what men we had in [the] Fort which I accordingly obeyed and find per the rolls that since the 15th instant, which was the day we began to fire from the Fort at the Enemy's batteries, the following men are fallen sick and not fit for service. . . . [Following this is] an account of what men we have had run away and deserted the garrison since 15 February 1689 which was the day the Sidi landed on Bombay to this day.[35]

[34] A subordinate commander. The term can also refer to a provincial governor.

[35] The names are left out of this edition for reasons of space. However, the results are shown in the following table:

	SICK AND UNFIT FOR SERVICE	DESERTED
First Company	9	18
Second Company	19	15
Third Company	6	14 including the Company sergeant
Fourth Company	17	16
From the ships		4
From the grenadiers (the governor's personal guard)		3
Others		A Company factor had also deserted.

The Portuguese gentlemen that went away over to the other side two or three days since to fetch supply is this day returned with about forty men.

March 26, 1689

The moon being in a thorough eclipse last night his Excellency ordered the guns to be fired at them [the Enemy] imagining that they might be gazing thereon. This day the General sent a present to Ram Rajah and the rest of the boats are gone to him for more supply. The spy that was brought into the Fort was this day delivered to the Savajees to use their own punishment upon, who immediately cut off his head, which they did at one blow. The Enemy firing at us and we at them continued all day.

March 27, 1689

This morning Captain Eaton sent the following list of his men ashore:

[This list is left out for reasons of space, but it listed fifty-eight men, of whom fifteen were sick and nine were "lame." Both the shore and ship musters suggest that epidemic disease, perhaps the plague, had reached the besieged town.]

Pasquall D'Lime of the 1st Company ran away and Daniel Horse of the 4th Company from his guard at the bunder. The Enemy having disabled by their shot one of our carriages upon the Tank Bastion his Excellency ordered it immediately to be mounted upon a new carriage, [during] the bringing up of which Anto Moreas of the 3rd Company received a cannon shot in his shoulder. This day we had a great many shot passed between one another and on board the battery ship we had two men wounded and one killed outright.

March 28, 1689

We continued firing at each other all day. Lieutenant Paul Paine continuing very ill went this day on board of [the hospital] ship.

March 29, 1689

This morning early the manchua, sloop [and sundry other] boats that went over to fetch supplies of men returned with about eighty men. His Excellency [was] expecting four or five hundred and sent this night said boats with Senhor Francis D'Mello, Dom St Paul who has promised to bring over the remainder which is about four hundred men more. We continued firing all day at each other. The Portuguese being very unkind will not suffer any of their men to embark off the Country,[36] so we are forced to march a great way about to the Savajee's Country [i.e., territory under Maratha control] which place is very shoaly and our boats lying off a vast way which occasioned the tediousness [i.e., long delays] in coming.

March 30, 1689

One John Swort and Gilbert Smith and Peter Johnson belonging to the 1st Company ran away from the Garrison and about 4 o-clock in the afternoon Captain Benjamin Stacy spied three of the Enemy's grabs[37] and went after them and engaged them.

March 31, 1689

About 10 o-clock this morning, having notice that the Enemy were in the woods behind the Company's garden, the Bandareens and Savajees went out to engage them. But they being overpowered by their number his Excellency ordered out Lieutenant Nangle that then commanded the out-guards who immediately engaged them. Then his Excellency ordered out Ensign Bryan Carney with eight files of men to their further assistance, and also Captain Gowen Ansley with ten files of men and Captain Barber about half an hour after with four files. And his Excellency himself being upon the Green[38] all the while ordering continually ammunition they engaged for nigh two hours very hotly. And about 11 o-clock his Excellency ordered me out with two files of grenadiers to Lieutenant Nangle to order him if they had beat them out of the woods to retreat, and when I came there they had beaten them out of the woods so all retreated. One of our Bandareens brought Sidi Ahmud's head to the General for which his Excellency gave him a piece of money for his encouragement in the service.[39] We lost not a man, only five

---

[36] From the territories and coasts they controlled. The Portuguese were trying to appear neutral in the conflict.

[37] ghorāb (Arabic) or gurāb (Marathi): In the seventeenth century, it referred to a medium-to-large two- or three-masted coastal or oceangoing vessel with a projecting prow, a broad beam, (generally) square-rigged sails, and high sides.

[38] The Bombay town common.

[39] See also entries for July 12 and November 6, 1689. The intent of this ghoulish exercise was to prove that a soldier or soldiers had killed a man of high rank.

wounded: one Domo. Fernand and Anto. Dupee of the 2d Company; Sergeant Minshall and Th[omas] Robinson of the 3d Company; and George Gray, Topass[40] of the 1st Company. His Excellency ordered eight Shiraz bottles of wine to the four Companies and twelve bottles to the parties that had been out upon service.

April 1, 1689

This day we were pretty quiet, only guns passing now and then at each other. We threw a shell out of our mortar piece into the yard of the East India House where they used to play a gun or two and believe it did great execution.

April 2, 1689

This morning Captain Benjamin Stacy brought this following account which happened between him and the Sidi's [forces] the 30th [of the] past month:

> Receiving a command from your Excellency to give a true and exact account of what happened between the Sidi and yacht Josiah I commence (vizt.)
>
> [On] March 30, 1689, about the hour [of] one in the afternoon, having received orders from your Excellency about some anchors, in pursuance of which order I made [out] four or five sail of large grabs to weigh from Mazagaon a-sailing toward Mahim. And knowing well that they could not get to Sion before the next flood [tide], I presumed to give them chase, hoping the Almighty would give me success. One of the grabs grounded on a sand[bar] something to the northward of Mole[41] [and] we came up with her, the tide of ebb being fallen some three foot. [However] we found we could not come to the other three grabs that, for fear of us, had grounded themselves on the pitch of high water near Chembur Point.[42] In consideration of which I anchored the yacht as near the first grounded grab as possibly I could, but finding that some twenty-seven of the Sidi's gallevats designed to protect the grab from the yacht, I immediately sent my boat on board of the first grab which our men found deserted and loaded with grain. Whereupon I ordered my men to come [back] on board of the yacht, knowing that we could not maintain the grab against the Sidi's gallevats. And to keep

---

[40] Generally, Christian Luso-Indians, though most commonly referring specifically to soldiers.

[41] A peninsula on the large island of Trombay, northeast of Bombay Island.

[42] Chembur Point was on the northwest shore of Trombay Island.

them from unlading her I veered the yacht aground within one third of a musket shot of her. The gallevats perceiving me aground came under our stern and fired their guns and small arms at us, but after we had brought our stern chaser[43] to fire on them they left us and boarded the grab. But we plying the small arms they quitted the grab and fell out of shot [i.e., passed out of range] of us.

About one in the morning there came in two squadrons with their drums and trumpets. [And] after they had engaged us one squadron boarded the grab and the other squadron lay firing on our starboard quarter. But we returning thanks for their salutes, they were pleased to leave the grab and joined the squadron on our starboard quarter with an intent to pass our broadside [so] as to relieve the three grabs that were aground whose men had deserted them. But as they endeavored to pass to the grabs we fired only three guns to give them their pass, whereupon they returned to Mazagaon as we suppose, for we never heard or saw them after. About an hour after [that] five Europe ships' boats came on board[44] in some of their boats. I desired [them] to carry two of my men on board of the grab and after [that] we jointly agreed to go with the five boats to the deserted grabs with this proviso: that if they found them remanned and mak[ing] stout resistance, to return to the yacht, for the advantage which high grabs has over low boats was considered.[45] What opposition they found I know not but if they had found hard service I do really believe they would have acted like true English men. But finding them [the grabs] not likely to float until the next spring [i.e., next high tide] [they] fired [i.e., set fire to] them all three. One in the morning we found not to be burnt quite down which we fired again. With the assistance of the five boats, we brought the yacht and one grab to wait your Excellency's command whom God preserve.

[The diary resumes.]

This morning also our boats that went over to the other side [i.e., over to the mainland] returned and brought with them 350 men to our support. About 11 o-clock firing a gun on the Plum Tree Bastion the gun split and wounded Mr. Gough, 2nd Mate of the Royal James and Mary and four men more, one of which was dangerously wounded. In the

---

[43] A gun mounted on the stern of a boat or ship.

[44] He presumably means the crews came on board.

[45] Grabs, mainly propelled by sails, had considerable tactical advantages over European longboats, which were designed to be rowed and were low to the water. In a grab, the men could fire down on any attackers, and the high sides of a grab made it hard for attackers to board.

evening about 6 or 7 o-clock the Padre Superior of Bandora[46] came to his Excellency from the Sidi by whom we had information that the yacht had sunk four of their gallevats.

April 3, 1689

This day after dinner the Padre that came yesterday from the Sidi returned to him with his Excellency's proposals.

April 4, 1689

Today his Excellency received a note from the Padre but found nothing material in it [answering] to his Excellency's reasonable proposals sent, notwithstanding the Sidi's courting to [the] Padre to come and treat [for peace]. And from the time of the Padre's coming there has been a cessation so his Excellency intends tomorrow to begin the war afresh.

April 5, 1689

This morning early the Padre Superior sent his servant to his Excellency to acquaint him [that] his master intended to wait upon him this morning, which he accordingly did about 11 o-clock, and brought with him the Sidi's proposals which his Excellency perused and in the evening sent his proposals per the Padre to the Sidi.

April 13, 1689

Ever since the 5th past we have had every day the Padre going and coming from and to us with articles between each other, but could not come to any agreement until this day when his Excellency fired five guns as a sign he accepted of the proposals that the Padre brought last night signed and sealed by the Sidi. And his Excellency also sent this day his proposals back by the said Padre which were also signed and sealed and in the afternoon they [the Enemy] fired five guns from their battery as a salute and acceptance of the same.

Yesterday Daniel Donavan, a grenadier, and Mat Mastin of the 1st Company ran away from the Garrison.

---

[46] This was the Father Superior of the Jesuit Mission in Bandora (now Bandra). The Jesuits resented the English presence at Bombay and therefore were prepared to make an alliance of convenience with the Sidi. However, they also acted as mediators and go-betweens at various points in the conflict. Bandora was on the southern tip of the large island of Salsette, separated from the Bombay archipelago by the Mahim River.

April 14, 1689

Yesterday Francis Hows belonging to the 2nd Company ran away from the Bunder Guard.

April 16, 1689

Samuel Smith of the 4th Company and James Mereday and Peter Bento of the 3rd Company ran away yesterday from the out-guards. His Excellency ordered our out-guards at the Judge's house and at the bunder should be relieved by the militia and that our farthest guards should be relieved by Sombooe's[47] party, which is the gentleman that brought over the men from the Portuguese country.

April 18, 1689

William Shaw, grenadier, ran away from the Garrison.

April 21, 1689

Captain Carr adviseth us from Mahim that the Emerald's boat going ashore on the 18th instant for some cows, Edward Gill ran away.

April 28, 1689

About noon Ensign Osboldiston died in the Fort.

April 29, 1689

Captain Richard Clifton departed this life.

May 8, 1689

His Honor Mr. Thomas Mitchell died on board the Royal James and Mary.

May 9, 1689

Mr. Daniel Edwards died also. This morning our Savajees and Bandareens going the rounds meet with a party of the Enemy who, falling out, engaged one another. His Excellency hearing them engaging in the woods ordered out Captain Gowen Ansley and Ensign Bryan Carney

---

[47] Here spelled "Sumboe," but Hilton elsewhere spells his name "Sombooe."

with seventeen files of men who also went and engaged the Enemy, the dispute being very hot for about the space of one hour, when [i.e., after which] the Enemy retreated to the bulwarks and our people retreated to the Fort. We had in this engagement Sergeant Minchin very dangerously wounded in the head and of all our party with the Savajees and Bandareens we had about thirty wounded and two or three killed outright.

May 16, 1689

His Excellency gave new colors, being yellow with the red cross to all the black[48] soldiery.

This afternoon the Sidi boats coming in Captain Gayer manned his boat who after some small time took one of them laden with grain.[49] His Excellency ordered that the quarter part thereof should be given to the men as an encouragement.

May 17, 1689

Sergeant John Wye who commands the manchua took [i.e., seized] another [supply] boat [belonging to the Sidi] laden with six cows, one calf and two sheep which his Excellency ordered to be brought to the Fort for the soldiery.

May 18, 1689

This day his Excellency having intelligence that the Sidi was at Mahim ordered our Savajees and Bandareens to go out and do what damage they could to the Enemy, who meet with the Enemy in the woods and had a very hot dispute for above an hour. When [i.e., Then] there came down from Mazagaon above four thousand men who, coming to their assistance, repulsed our people, so his Excellency ordered out Ensign Bryan Carney with the Militia who went up very briskly and beat them back again. Then was ordered out Lieutenant Arthur Nangle with eight files of men; when [i.e., from that time] they engaged the Enemy until it was dark night, so all retreated to their respective quarters. In the time

---

[48] In the diary, the term "black" always refers to South Asians. When the diarist wants to refer to sub-Saharan Africans (which included the Sidis as well as local enslaved and free people of African origin), he uses the term "Coffree" (from the Arabic kāfir, meaning unbeliever or infidel).

[49] In other words, some enemy supply boats were spotted, and Captain Gayer's men succeeded in capturing one of them at sea.

of the engagement his Excellency ordered some of the Fort guns to be fired at their battery; they [the Enemy] fired from his Honor's house at the battery ships, but not a gun at the Fort. We had Lieutenant Arthur Nangle mortally wounded and three English men more killed outright and several of the Militia and Savajees wounded.

May 19, 1689

This morning our Bandareens and Savajees (going into the woods per his Excellency's order to see if they could find any of our dead that was killed in yesterday's skirmish) they found one Isaac Scott (lying wounded) who formerly ran to the Sidi from the Bunder Guard, and being brought before a Court Martial confessed that he had entered himself in the Sidi's service and that he had fired several great guns against us. There is several witnesses against him that see him in the last skirmish (being on Sunday the 12th instant) at the very head of the Enemy firing at our party several times, and he having little to say for himself, the whole body of the Court declared that he ought to die and be hanged up immediately out of hand, he being taken in actual service and arms against his King and Country. Sentence was passed that he be hanged by the neck until his body is dead dead dead, and so Lord have mercy on his soul.[50] And this sentence was accordingly executed on the said Scott by the Provost Martial hanging him on a gibbet prepared for that purpose being fastened to the angle gun[51] on the Tank Bastion where he hung from 9 o'clock in the morning until sunset for a spectacle and warning to such inhuman criminals.

Between 11 and 12 o'clock at night Lieutenant Nangle died of his wound he received in yesterday's skirmish.

May 21, 1689

This day arrived here the Kempthorne, Captain John Kempthorne, Commander, directly from England who brought ninety soldiers and two mortar pieces.

May 22, 1689

Arrived here also the Diana, Captain Charles Masters, Commander, who brought us thirty soldiers and good supply of powder and ammunition.

---

[50] The incantatory phrase "hanged by the neck until his body is dead dead dead, and so Lord have mercy on his soul" was the traditional form of the sentence of death in English courts.

[51] Perhaps a howitzer.

May 25, 1689

At night his Excellency having advice that the Enemy's boats was come from Danda-Rajpuri[52] ordered all the Europe commanders to get their men-of-war boats in readiness. Captain Roger Carr, having that day brought in a prize boat, and lying over beyond all the shipping, espied them coming so fired some guns which alarmed the whole fleet, so all our boats went off and came up with the Enemy's boats and had a very hot engagement. And at length [our boats] took two of the [enemy's] boats and killed them about two or three-hundred men and brought several others [as] prisoners to the Fort whereof sixteen were dangerously wounded which his Excellency released and set them at liberty.

May 26, 1689

This evening came hither the Padre Superior of Bandora with Senhor Xavier De Soaza with letters from the Captain General of the North.[53] Also this day Captain Benjamin Stacy and Captain Benson brought in a prize boat.

May 30, 1689

His Excellency ordered Sombooe to entrench and build a bulwark round about the Moody's house[54] which is now in agitation.

June 8, 1689

One Goslin being in the Josiah Frigate's boat astern was drove away by stress of weather and no news of either boat or man can be heard of. Our Bandareens and Savajees being in the woods gathering coconuts espied the Enemy approaching towards them, which [made] them to put themselves in a posture of defense. And the Enemy coming up [they] engaged one another very hotly and after some time Rama Comotin[55] came to the

---

[52] The stronghold of the Sidis down the coast from Bombay, where they also maintained their famous island fortress of Janjira.

[53] The Captain General of the North, João de Sequeira e Faria, ruled a string of Portuguese coastal towns north of Goa. He played an important role in brokering the eventual peace deal between the East India Company and the envoys from Surat and the Mughal emperor (Document 17).

[54] A moody (modi in several South Asian languages) was a grain merchant or grocer.

[55] Rama Comotin (or Kámáti) — in the original, Ramajee Commattee — had been a fairly prominent figure at Bombay, his family having owned the tax farm on tobacco prior to the war; he and his brother also acquired a lot of land seized from deserters following the war, though he fell into some political trouble with a subsequent governor of the island, who attempted to have his lands dispossessed. In 1720, he was convicted, based

General and told him that the Enemy overpowered our black soldiery and pressed his Excellency to send them recruit[s]. When [i.e., Accordingly,] with [i.e., after] much importunities [the General] sent Ensign Bryan Carney and Ensign John FitzGerald with a party of men who, as soon as coming up with the Enemy and firing thick amongst them, forced them to retreat. And on a sudden a violent shower of rain forcing our party to the run [they] came home with the loss of five men.[56]

His Excellency considering that it would be convenient to build caserns[57] for to keep the soldiers in the Garrison from the violence of the weather, ordered just before the rains set in that there should a convenient place be built within the Fort for each Company, which was done accordingly: the First Company being quartered in a casern in the Fort yard, the 2d Company being in a shed on the Plum Tree Bastion to the Lower Bastion, and the 4th Company on the curtain between the Lower Bastion and the Flagstaff Bastion. Also over the gateway was a conveniency built for sentinels that they might always be there. His Excellency's Guard of Grenadiers were quartered under the long gallery in the lower warehouses.

June 16, 1689

John Essington of his Excellency's Guard of Grenadiers ran away from the Garrison.

June 20, 1689

John Scott of the 3d Company ran away.

June 24, 1689

His Excellency in the morning receiving advice that the Enemy was, with a vast number of his men, approaching towards us ordered out all our black soldiery to meet them in the woods, who when met had a hot dispute. One party of the Enemy were got into tanks [i.e., water reservoirs] all which we soon perceived from the Fort and so gave them several great guns which routed them thence to Lieutenant Nangle's house. Which we perceiving, plied our guns hotly there and soon dis-

---

on evidence that was later discredited, of conspiring with the Maratha "pirate" Kanhoji Angre; he was imprisoned, and his estates were confiscated. He died in 1728.

[56] It was the beginning of the monsoon season.

[57] Caserns ("case arms" in the original) were temporary shelters built to house soldiers and their weapons, usually built close by where they were stationed.

persed them. Lieutenant Peter Edwards was ordered out with fourteen files of men to assist the black soldiers and sometime afterwards the General ordered me out with his Guard of Grenadiers to Lieutenant Edwards' assistance if occasion required. And as I was coming up by the English Church [I] meet the Enemy driving our black people before them, where I engaging them they retreated back. Then his Excellency ordered out Lieutenant Carney who met with the Enemy and totally routed them. This day we lost not one Englishman and but one Savajee; some few wounded.

June 25, 1689

His Excellency being advised that one of these dark nights the Enemy had an intent to storm the Fort, therefore in order to receive them he ordered the flanker guns[58] to be laden with partridge and round shot and all the powder chests on the several bastions and curtains to have one barrel of powder and other ammunition equivalent thereto.

June 26, 1689

His Excellency ordered that there should be prepared lights made of pitch, tar, dammar[59] and other ingredients which were to be hung on the walls as also lanterns and [other such] conveniencies of lighting us, to be ready upon all occasions. And [he] also ordered and caused to be hung up at the gateway and likewise gave a paper of orders to every respective commission officer for the quarters of every individual person within the Fort and ordered stones to be placed on the walls round the Fort.

June 28, 1689

His Excellency receiving advice that the Sidi had promised great rewards to his people in case they would attack the Fort and in pursuance to his promise had ordered three hundred gold maneloes[60] and six hundred silver to be made, which would give one to each man that should storm the Fort. And [the Sidi] had already given to his captains which he had pitched on [i.e., chosen] to storm the Fort gold maneloes.

---

[58] Guns overlooking a potential line of assault.
[59] Dammar was a combustible type of tree gum.
[60] Likely referring to a "manilha," a bracelet or armlet.

He intends also to attack us by sea and so to land with his gallevats at the Lower Bastion.

June 29, 1689

About 3 o-clock in the morning the Enemy came and alarmed our Guards, the Captain of which party was killed by our out-guards which occasioned their no nigher [i.e., closer] approach (as we believe) at that time.[61]

July 2, 1689

Domingo Mendizo belonging to the 4th Company going beyond his bounds was by a party of the Enemy seized and by force carried away. We had advice from the Portuguese that on [the] 25th [of] last month we threw one of our bombs which fell into the battery which was [formerly] the President's house, which killed of the Enemy about thirty men and wounded fifty-two men which came over to the Portuguese Country to be cured of their wounds being most of them very desperate.

July 12, 1689

Mr. Edward Cornwall, Mr. Bathurst, Captain Barber, Mr. Thurscross and some others going down to Sombooe's Battery at the Moody's house to try a piece or two [aimed] at their [the Enemy's] battery, and firing saw nobody [so they] went towards the bazaar. And looking up and down one Edward Melville espied a party of the Enemy sitting smoking the hubble bubble[62] so he fired at them. They all rising up, Captain Barber and the rest had a fair shot at them. We engaged one another until the black people were sent out to assist them who engaged some time until the Enemy sent down his whole forces upon them, the Enemy being very numerous. [Thereupon was] ordered out Lieutenant Paul Paine with twelve files of men who had a very hot dispute together [for] some time, the Enemy coming quite down to Sombooe's Battery. Then his Excellency ordered out Captain Jacob Barber with the grenadiers to go and secure Sombooe's Battery, most of his [Sombooe's] men being engaged in other places. The grenadiers firing smartly out of the battery made them [i.e., the enemy] presently retreat and Captain Barber and

---

[61] It prevented them from coming any closer.
[62] An onomatopoeic term for a hookah (water pipe).

the grenadiers ran into the bazaar after them so that they totally routed the several parties. After a dispute which held from 10 in the morning till 3 in the afternoon our people brought in two heads one whereof [is] supposed and believed to be some great man's.[63] Besides we are certain [we] have done them great damage without the loss of one man (many of our black people being wounded) and Sergeant Coye belonging to the grenadiers shot in the thigh. Only Sombooe, a brave man, after the fight was over coming to pay his respects to the Governor, and in his way to his quarters as he was returning, an unlucky shot from the battery took off his leg of which wound he in half an hour deceased.

July 14, 1689

We had advice from the Portuguese that on the 12th instant in our last engagement we killed outright of the Enemy no less than [left blank] and wounded them at least [left blank] [and] that there is three great Captains [killed or badly wounded] which wore gold maneloes which were given them by the Sidi the name[s] whereof are [left blank]. We are also informed that this day there went away about 350 men at least (and two palanquins)[64] from the Sidi and the Enemy much discouraged.

July 15, 1689

Captain Barber and some others went out into the bazaar and seeing some of the Enemy fired at them. They also fired some few pieces [back] again; one of them shot one William Ardis into the belly, of which wound he presently died. But the Enemy retreated.

July 17, 1689

John Maul belonging to the 2d Company ran away to the Sidi.

July 20, 1689

[There] came one Evert Evertson from the Mughal's army to serve his Excellency, who formerly being by profession a chirurgeon [i.e., surgeon], his Excellency ordered him to assist Dr. Stavely in the hospital.

---

[63] A top commander or noble, or both.
[64] Covered litters or sedan chairs used by men and women of high rank.

July 25, 1689

The two subadars who left his Excellency's service some days before at some disgust [i.e., grievance] this day returned from Karanja[65] and begged his Excellency's pardon, withal desiring to be entertained again [i.e., taken into service again]. His Excellency was pleased to grant it.

July 26, 1689

About 2 o-clock in the afternoon went out our black soldiery into the woods as they had done several times since the last engagement (but the Enemy never durst come out) to meet the Enemy who at last came out and engaged our people. When [i.e., At which time] his Excellency, hearing them engaging hot, ordered out Lieutenant Bryan Carney with twelve files of Europeans who also went up and immediately engaged, as also Ensign William Magregory with the Militia which were not above three files of men, and after them [his Excellency] ordered ammunition by some of his own Guard of Grenadiers. All which engaging the Enemy very hotly and had hard service, the Enemy being numerous, they [the Enemy] having at least forty European[s] in the field (which formerly deserted our Garrison, most of which fell upon our grenadiers and called out to them by their names). 'Tis most certain we have done them great damage but as yet unknown [i.e., unconfirmed]. But our people saw several of their people fall, particularly taking notice of one man (supposed to be a great person) who was carried off by a palanquin as soon as he fell. We also received damage enough, for we had four Europeans wounded and one Frognell, a grenadier, killed outright, five or six black fellows killed and six or seven wounded.

But however we forced them to quit the field and then our black people came away up to the Judge's house, where his Excellency was walking on that part of the Green being most secure from the Enemy's great shot. And when the captains were making their salaams there to his Excellency (believing the Enemy might have [had] some intelligence thereof) they [the Enemy] fired a whole culverin[66] which took the house just in the middle, which made the dust fly into his Excellency's face but did no other hurt. Europeans wounded: Thomas Cooper, grenadier, shot in the arm; Francis Draper through the thigh; Joseph Good-

---

[65] In original, "Karinjah": an island to the southeast of Bombay, en route to the mainland.
[66] A large cannon.

man in the face; Henderick Arnee wounded in the head and Sergeant Michael George shot through the pectoral muscle.

July 29, 1689

His Excellency had advice from the Portuguese that for a certain [i.e., for certain] on the 26th instant we did the Enemy very great damage and that Pillajee, a potent [i.e., powerful] Captain, with three or four more potent Captains were slain and that the Sidi himself was wounded in the leg.

August 2, 1689

One Rowlandson of the 1st Company ran away to the Sidi.

August 7, 1689

Captain Benjamin Stacy sending his gallevat (which he desired of the General for to cruise up and down) last night toward Mazagaon with twelve men in her who, happening to fall asleep, the Sidi in the night sent off a boat and took them all except two men who leapt overboard. The one swam to the yacht and the other toward Cross Island, who was taken up by our guard-boat and carried on board the yacht.

August 9, 1689

About 12 at noon our Bandareens and Savajees went out toward the Enemy who presently came out and engaged one another very hotly. His Excellency ordered out Lieutenant Bryan Carney with twelve files of the Garrison soldiers who coming up [found] the Enemy had took possession of a wall that belonged to Lieutenant Nangle's house and garden, which [meant] our people could see nothing of them. And they all the time firing through loop-holes they had made for that purpose at us, in which engagement we had six men wounded and one killed outright; his Excellency now having given order that Lieutenant Nangle's wall be pulled down to the ground that the Enemy may no more shelter there.

August 10, 1689

Our black people went out and leveled the wall according to order.

August 12, 1689

About 10 o-clock in the morning the Admiral hoisted his ensign seeing some vessels out at sea, but we not having taken notice thereof at the

Fort, Captain Cooke's boat came ashore about 5 o-clock in the afternoon and brought his Excellency word that they [had] made [out] two ships, two grabs and two gallevats out at sea. Whereupon his Excellency immediately ordered out the Ruby, Emerald and Josiah Frigates as also the manchua with nine files of men from the Garrison commanded by Ensign Magregory to make the best of their way to them, and in case they prove our Enemy, to take, burn, sink or destroy them if possible. And sometime after [his Excellency] ordered three gallevats to be manned with three files of men more to go after them.

August 15, 1689

His Excellency toward the evening (we having all the day been firing great guns at each other) ordered a couple of bombs to be played, one at the Portuguese Church and another at the battery which they were then raising at the old large warehouse near the Low Battery at the President's house, both which fell very well, one falling into the Portuguese Church to our views and the other touched the very wall of the battery house as we designed.

August 16, 1689

His Excellency ordered the guns to be fired at the new battery which they [the Enemy] were then erecting which we continued for half the day and believe did much mischief.

August 18, 1689

In the morning Captain Benjamin Stacy sent word in a letter to his Excellency that the Sidi with most of his forces were gone up to Mahim upon which news his Excellency gave orders for all our black soldiery to go out and do all the mischief they could and also ordered out Lieutenant Bryan Carney and Ensign FitzGerald with sixteen files of men, one being to take possession of the Sessions House and the other Lieutenant Nangle's house which they accordingly performed. But our black people after some hot dispute ran away[67] so that Lieutenant Carney and Ensign FitzGerald were forced to retreat, yet did the Enemy some visible damage. A party of Bandareens which his Excellency had given positive orders to keep with the main body went straggling down

---

[67] It is unclear whether this "dispute" was an engagement with the enemy or a dispute between the "black soldiers" and Carney and FitzGerald.

toward the bay where a parcel of Pathans[68] meet them and cut most of them off and others were forced into the sea which was their own faults in not obeying orders.

August 19, 1689

His Excellency dispatched away the Shrewsbury, Emerald, Ruby and Josiah Frigates with orders to cruise to the Northward and destroy, take and annoy the Enemy as much as in them lay [i.e., as much as they could]. Also that day his Excellency had Information that the Enemy was fortifying the Sessions House[69] and by reason they work in the night ordered the guns to be plied at the Sessions House all night long each half hour.

August 21, 1689

In the morning our black soldiers went out and had taken possession of the Sessions House and alarmed all the forces and made them come down from Mazagaon, but it beginning to rain very hard they came away to their quarters we firing great guns at each other most part of the day.

August 23, 1689

We threw two shells [between] about 4 and 5 in the evening one whereof did visible execution, killing two men which were standing just without the battery at the warehouse. And about 8 o-clock at night the Enemy alarmed us thinking to surround the Moody's house firing also three or four great guns out of their battery at the warehouse, but our people firing hotly out of the Moody's house the Enemy retreated and we were very quiet all night long. When on the morrow our black people went out and alarmed the Enemy and had about one or two hours' engagement, but it raining extremely violent were forced to retreat each to their respective quarters.

August 25, 1689

At night [between] about 10 & 11 the sentinel of the Lower Bastion gave notice of the Enemy going or coming from the battery ships that lay

---

[68] The Pathans were a semi-nomadic people from what is now Afghanistan and western Pakistan (in modern times, they are more often referred to as Pashtuns). They had a formidable reputation as fighters and were in high demand as military labor.
[69] The Sessions House was the courthouse and prison; before the siege, it was one of the largest buildings in the town of Bombay. It was largely destroyed in the fighting.

unmanned. But his Excellency firing some great guns and sending out the guard-boats which went to the said battery ships they [the Enemy] were gone.

August 26, 1689

In the morning between 9 and 10 returned our manchua from Chaul;[70] his Excellency ordering the same day five gallevats to go over toward Trombay[71] cruising thereabouts, one whereof being manned with Savajees. One Alexander Colhoune belonging to the 1st Company was put in command thereof who taking his opportunity left the boat and deserted the Garrison.

August 28, 1689

In the morning was a fleet of boats seen standing in from the S[ea?]. Upon which his Excellency immediately ordered out all the Europe ships' boats, manchua and our gallevats which went out in pursuance of them and brought them into our bay before the evening.

August 29, 1689

In the morning his Excellency ordered the men (being two Portuguese that were taken per the fleet) that were brought in yesterday. And after having examined them very strictly, and not having any proof but that they belonged to the Portuguese, thought fit immediately to discharge them.

George Manuell's Declaration:

George Manuell being three or four days since at Bandora and saw several coolies that were intended to come and serve the English at Bombay, but were imprisoned for the same intent by the Padre Superior of the place, who asked them in the hearing of the deponent why they would go and serve dogs. He further says that the Bandora people told him that the said Padre Superior sold to the Sidi sixty morahs of batty[72] and that he received for the same coconuts and ten xeraphins[73]

---

[70] Chaul was a Portuguese town on the mainland about sixty kilometers south of Bombay. It was the most important city between Bombay and the Sidis' stronghold of Danda-Rajpuri.

[71] Trombay was a large island to the northeast of Bombay. Its southern coastline was directly opposite Mazagaon where the Sidi had his base of operations during the siege.

[72] A morah was a measure of dry volume; batty is rice.

[73] The xeraphin was a silver coin current in the Portuguese settlements worth about 1 shilling, 6–8 pence.

per thousand and that the Sidi has sent to the said Padre for a supply of powder, balls, money, and [such like] all which it is said the Padre furnished him with. And that he [the Padre] is very angry with the people of Bandora who endeavored to hinder a boat of plantains which came from Versera[74] or some other place being sold to the Sidis, he asking the people why they should deny the Sidi of such refreshment. He [Manuell] further declareth [he] being sent to Bandora per his Excellency to raise soldiers to serve in our Garrison, which, when he had raised twenty-four men out of that place, the Padre Superior, having notice thereof, immediately ordered two of them to be imprisoned and likewise said that whatsoever persons of that place should go to serve the English or any other nation they should be imprisoned upon it, and the man never to have habitation there anymore. He [Manuell] also says that the people of Kurli[75] that were sent by the Padre of that place to supply the Sidi with rice, being exacted upon [perhaps defrauded?] by the Sidis, refused to go any more. Upon that the said Padre forced them to go back again and sell it as formerly.

[The diary resumes.]

His Excellency in the night was taken with an extreme fit of the colic and about 2 o-clock in the morning [we] were forced to open the gates that the doctor of the Berkeley Castle might be let in, he being sent for to his Excellency.

September 1, 1689

Captain Masters sent in a boat that he took upon suspicion, they pretending they were going to Karanja to get salt. And coming before the Court they proved to be Portuguese so were again dismissed. Also Mr. George Weldon, Mr. Barker Hibbins and Mr. Abraham Navarro set out for Bassein[76] there to meet the merchants to know their last result and what will be done as to an accommodation.[77]

---

[74] Perhaps Versova, a fishing and agricultural town on Salsette.

[75] Kurli was a village on the island of Salsette. It was under Portuguese rule in the seventeenth century. Today it is known as Kurla.

[76] Bassein was a fortified port town north of Bombay, belonging to the Portuguese (the Portuguese name was "Baçaim").

[77] This was an attempt to work out the terms of a peace. For further details, see Document 17.

September 2, 1689

Story Hawkins, belonging to the Garrison and being ordered on board the Josiah Frigate this day, ran away from the said frigate and has deserted the Garrison.

The Enemy from the great warehouse (where is now mounted six guns) shot through Captain Hilder's house in which house was one English man, two black women and a Topass, the former being wounded, one woman killed outright, and the other wounded.

September 3, 1689

John Davison belonging to the 2nd Company, being ordered sometime since on board the yacht [and] being drunk, last night fell overboard and was drowned.

September 4, 1689

This day sailed out of the Road[78] the New Berkeley Castle for England; in her ballast [left blank].

September 5, 1689

Our gallevats brought in two boats one whereof has a Portuguese pass and the other proving not to be an Enemy were immediately dismissed.

September 6, 1689

We fired several guns at the Enemy and received the like from them and about 4 o-clock in the afternoon the Enemy threw a stone out of their battery[79] which fell upon the Prince's Bastion[80] and killed one Dennis Giblin belonging to the 4th Company. In the evening we threw two shells at the Enemy one whereof broke behind their battery in the tank and the other at the foot of their battery on the hill which did no visible execution. And firing some great guns a little time after on the Company's Bastion[81] one of them split and wounded three of our montrosses,[82] one whereof had a thigh and a leg broke and the other two much splintered.

---

[78] A sheltered stretch of water near the shore "where vessels may lie at anchor in safety" (OED).

[79] This probably means that the Sidis had fired a mortar. Using shaped stones instead of cannon balls was common in this period.

[80] The Prince's Bastion was a landward-facing bastion.

[81] The location of this bastion is unclear.

[82] A montross is a gunner's mate or assistant.

September 7, 1689

This day we had one Garett Direckson and Augustin Vandurin belonging to the 4th Company ran away, they both belonging to the Josiah Frigate.

September 8, 1689

One William Watson, drummer, belonging to the 4th Company, ran away to the Enemy and one of our black soldiers going behind Mr. Harbin's house was met with by a party of the Enemy who tied him to a tree and cut off his right hand and so let him come back, but the said black man said he saw the drummer go voluntarily away with them.

September 9, 1689

Came a party of men from Ram Rajah consisting of about sixty men with letters to his Excellency from the said Ram Rajah so [we] daily expect more recruits.

September 10, 1689

About 12 o-clock at noon our black people went out and met with the Enemy in the woods who engaged one another very hotly for the space of three hours. When [i.e., Then] about 2 o-clock in the afternoon his Excellency ordered Mr. George Cooke and Mr. Cornwall to go down to be without the gate (himself being indisposed) to give orders for ammunition and [the like]. Lieutenant Peter Edwards and Ensign William Magregory were ordered out with a party of the garrison soldiers, but before they came up the black people and our great guns from the Fort had beat the Enemy off so that there was no occasion for them proceeding. There was one head brought into the Fort which was said to be a Captain of the Sidi's being a Coffree.[83] In the day's action we visibly did the Enemy great mischief and we had about thirty of our black soldiers wounded and one or two killed outright.

September 11, 1689

One James Cable belonging to his Excellency's Guard of Grenadiers ran away.

---

[83] This is the most explicit reference in the diary to the fact that the Sidis were of African origin.

September 12, 1689

About 10 o-clock at night there came out of Mazagaon fifteen or sixteen gallevats which, meeting with our guard-boats, engaged one another until about 4 o-clock in the morning. In the skirmish we came off very clear without hurt and forced their boats to retreat to the fort at Mazagaon.

September 14, 1689

This day his Excellency ordered the manchua and four gallevats to go towards Mazagaon to cruise. [He] also ordered all the Europe ships' boats to go every night to lie near the yacht to be ready to prevent the Enemy's boats going out or coming into the island. About 9 o-clock this morning a shot from the Enemy's battery took away one leg and one arm of one of our coolies who died in four hours' time.

September 16, 1689

One Patrick Willson belonging to the 2d Company ran away. This night our boats going towards Mazagaon (as usual) meet with the Enemy's boats who engaged very hotly from 8 to 12, we having in the skirmish but one man wounded (belonging to Captain Barber).

September 17, 1689

The Enemy raised palmares[84] against the Sessions House in order to [unreadable: fortify it(?)].

September 18, 1689

The General ordered our black soldiers to go out and alarm the Enemy which about 11 at night they accordingly went out, as also our ships' boats as well as our manchua. Six gallevats were ordered to go out under the command of Captain Jacob Barber, his Excellency having advice that some of the Enemy's boats lay laden at Mahim. And about 11 at night we heard great firing as we believe up as high as Sion, Mahim and [the like places].

---

[84]The palmare, or palmyra, locally known as brab, is a wild palm tree. The Sidis and later the English used lengths of board from these hardy trees to reinforce their batteries and earthworks.

September 19, 1689

This morning about 11 o-clock our black soldiers went out and proceeded so far as Lieutenant Nangle's house where they fired [i.e., set fire to] several houses that the Enemy used to lodge in, the Enemy not coming out but fired several great guns at them. One whereof from the Sessions House killed three and wounded three more, upon which our people came in. His Excellency being without the gate a considerable time and coming in to rest himself at the Judge's house opposite to the Fort gate, one of the Enemy's shot hit against the curtain of the Company Bastion of [which a part] broke off. Which one piece came directly in at the door where his Excellency was sitting and struck the wall near where he sat, but did no damage, there being in the same room Mr. Cooke, Lieutenant Carney, two grenadiers and several Portuguese. This afternoon about 4 o-clock Captain Barber came in and gave the following account: that going with the ships' boats, manchua and gallevats as his Excellency had ordered through the Inward Channel, the Josiah's long boat (unluckily) grounded [i.e., ran aground] at Sion, which alarmed the Enemy who fired great and small shot very briskly at them and our boats at them again. And having got her [the longboat] off [they] went for Mahim but found no boats there but received several shot from the Enemy ashore and returned the like again, but (praised be God) in this enterprise had not a man wounded nor received any damage from the Enemy.

September 23, 1689

From the 19th instant to this day the Enemy hath fired several shot at us, as likewise we at him again (but praised be God) we have received no damage. This day Captain Wale Commander of the Charles and John died.

September 24, 1689

This day his Excellency ordered the Josiah Frigate to go up to Surat river's mouth[85] and likewise ordered the Jonas, Captain Benson, with the manchua and six gallevats to go and lie at Mahim (being very well manned and provided with all things necessary) for to hinder the Enemy's

---

[85] Surat lay slightly inland on the River Tapti. The deepwater port was therefore at the river's mouth.

boats either going from or coming to the Island and to annoy them all they can.

September 28, 1689

From the 24th instant to this day several shot have passed between the Enemy and us, but (praised be God) have received no damage and uncertain what the Enemy may have received. This day arrived the Emerald Frigate [back] from cruising and brought in with her a grab laden with coconuts and [such like] but she being by a Court of Admiralty[86] not found to be our Enemy was cleared and another small boat found to be a prize. One [name left blank] came from the Mughal's army who formerly ran from the [East India ship] Modena at Basra and turned Turk.[87]

September 29, 1689

One Evert Evertson, a Dutchman that lately came from the Mughal's army to us together with one Jonathan Sewell, being both assistants to the Doctor, ran away to the Sidi.

September 30, 1689

One Richard Ball belonging to the 3d Company ran away, whereupon his Excellency ordered that there should be no Fort liberty granted.

October 1, 1689

His Excellency and Council ordered the soldiery to be in arms and about 7 o-clock in the morning came down, when [i.e., at which time] his Excellency made a speech to the soldiers and then gave [i.e., administered] an oath first to his Council, commission officers, factors, writers, and [sundry others], as also all the soldiers particularly, the tenor of which oath was to be true to their King and Country as also to the Right Honorable [East India] Company and this present General or his successors. Also to their being true to stand by and defend the Garrison and not desert it, etc., which every man particularly took. And

---

[86] In 1683, the East India Company had received patents from Charles II, which were renewed in 1686 by James II, to hold courts, primarily to judge prizes (i.e., determine the legality and value of ships and goods captured at sea). For details, see Document 4.

[87] Basra was a port on the Persian Gulf that was part of the Ottoman Empire; today it is part of Iraq. The reference to the sailor having "turned Turk" means that he had converted to Islam.

after all was done his Excellency sent for a bottle of wine and drank his Majesty's health and ordered that every man that had taken [the oath] should drink it at his Excellency's charge.

October 3, 1689

Yesterday some shot passed between the Enemy and us but we received no [damage] and are uncertain what damage might do the Enemy. This day Captain Benson sent in a grab as a prize by John Wood, Corporal of the Grenadiers. And about 7 o-clock in the evening the cadjan houses under Caesar's Bastion[88] and curtain were set on fire, whether by treachery or accident is not known. But it burnt about twenty of those small hovels and did no other hurt as it pleased God. The Enemy perceiving us to be on fire very near the Fort fired several great shot at those who were about to put it out but did no damage.

October 5, 1689

Yesterday the Enemy fired at us and we at him again but we received no [damage] and are uncertain what damage may have done the Enemy. Towards the evening, perceiving the Enemy had put up a barricade [a]cross the mouth of the bazaar, his Excellency ordered the black soldiers to go out and pull it down. And also the Enemy were about fortifying Lieutenant Nangle's house, but our black people going briskly up frighted them thence.

October 6, 1689

Our black people went out towards Lieutenant Nangle's house where the Enemy had taken possession and when they came up with them they fired but could not get them out, until our great guns at the Fort plying very hot upon the said house, the Enemy deserted it and ran away to their quarters.

October 8, 1689

Yesterday several guns [i.e., exchanges of fire] passed between the Enemy and us but we received no damage and are uncertain what the Enemy may have received. This evening, perceiving the Enemy was at work at Lieutenant Nangle's house, we fired our great guns at the

---

[88] This bastion possibly became what was later known as the Old Mandvi Bastion.

house and so continued firing all the night each half hour one or two guns, which hindered the Enemy that night.

October 9, 1689

We fired two bombs, one whereof fell into the Enemy's battery at his Honor's house, which we supposed did them great damage.

October 11, 1689

Yesterday the Enemy fired at us and we likewise at him again, but we received no [damage] and know not what damage might do them. This day one Story Hawkins and Patrick Willson who were some time before either taken or ran away, came and surrendered themselves to the black soldiers at Mr. Stanley's house (it being late in the evening) and on the next morning were brought to the Fort. His Excellency being on board the Royal James and Mary they were examined by the Deputy Governor, they saying they being drunk were taken by the Sidi's people in the woods. So having the opportunity [they] came [back] again and further say that several of our men to the number of sixty or thereabouts are with the Sidi, whereof above thirty are turned Moors[89] and that the Sidi, at their first being brought before him, asked them several questions relating to the affairs of the Garrison. But they were at this time put by until his Excellency's further orders.

October 12, 1689

This day Captain Benson was ordered down from Mahim and Captain Masters ordered to lie in his berth [i.e., to take his place].

October 13, 1689

This day Sergeant John Kew brought in a shybar[90] from off of Mahim as a prize.

October 14, 1689

Captain William Halford arrived from the Shrewsbury, Ruby and Emerald who sent in a grab as a prize. [He] also brought news that Captain Harrison, Commander of the Emerald Frigate, was very ill.

---

[89] "Turned Moors" means the men have converted to Islam.
[90] A large coastal transport ship with one, two, or three masts.

October 16, 1689

Yesterday and today likewise several shot have passed between the Enemy and us, but we received no damage and are uncertain what they may have received. This day the shybar as Sergeant Kew brought in as a prize on the 13th instant, was examined by a Court of Admiralty and not proving [to be] our Enemy's was cleared.

October 17, 1689

This day our people began to fortify at Captain Thorburn's house and being at work about 2 o-clock in the morning, the Sidi sent down a party of about a thousand men, but our black people stood to it and beat them back with only one man on our side being wounded.

October 19, 1689

Yesterday the Enemy fired at us and we at him but we received no damage and are uncertain what they may have received. This day the Enemy fired two small guns out of their new battery at Lieutenant Nangle's house at our new battery at Captain Thorburn's, one whereof took [off] the top of a palmare but did no hurt.

October 21, 1689

Yesterday several shot passed between us and the Enemy but we received no damage and are uncertain what he may have received. This day we perceived the Enemy to come down from Mazagaon in great numbers which caused us to suspect that they would alarm us but notwithstanding they were very quiet and no attempt offered that night.

October 22, 1689

About 2 or 3 o-clock in the afternoon Captain Barber, Lieutenant Carney, Mr. Thurscross and Captain Halford and several other gentlemen, going out found our black Christian soldiers engaging the Enemy in the Bay on the back side of the woods, who when they [the Englishmen] came up with them fired also at them very briskly. But the Enemy lay skulking under banks and in holes [so] that they could not do any great damage to them. We had three men wounded, one whereof was a servant to Mr. George Cooke, who had a ball placed in his neck and thought to be dangerous.

October 24, 1689

Yesterday passed some shot between the Enemy and us but we received no damage and are uncertain what might do the Enemy. This day the Enemy threw three stones, all [of] which fell into the Fort, one of them breaking through the shed where the grenadiers are quartered and lit upon Sergeant Mumford's cot and had he not been called off and made good haste it had certainly killed him.

October 25, 1689

One John Spencer belonging to the 1st Company ran away from Sergeant Samuel Jones' boat at Bandora, so over at Mahim and went to the Enemy. This day also the Jonas, Captain Benson, Commander, and the Josiah Frigate, Captain William Halford, Commander, and a shybar were ordered to go down the Coast, Captain Benson for Calicut[91] and Captain Halford for Karwar.[92]

October 30, 1689

From the 25th instant to this day the Enemy hath continued firing his great guns and firing stones at us, several whereof lit in the Fort and likewise we at him but (praised be God) hath done us no harm but are uncertain what we may have done the Enemy. And this day his Excellency ordered out the manchua and six gallevats upon an expedition; the Savajees having likewise manned out six boats to their assistance. This afternoon passed by the Portuguese Armada and came in one Curry Curry with arrack.[93]

November 1, 1689

About 5 o-clock in the evening the Enemy flung three stones, none of which lit in the Fort, but one in the Moody's Battery but did no damage.

---

[91] Calicut is on the southwestern coast of India in the present-day state of Kerala. In the medieval and early modern periods, it was an important spice port. It should not be confused with Calcutta, a city in eastern India inland from the Bay of Bengal.

[92] Karwar was a trading port just south of Portuguese Goa on the west coast of India. It traded in cotton muslin, pepper, cardamom, and other commodities. The English East India Company had an important factory there.

[93] An alcoholic drink distilled from palm wine.

November 2, 1689

This day the manchua and gallevats returned having met with twelve of the Sidi's boats which ran ashore and were hauled up under a battery so that our boats could not come at them, but fired smartly at one another. We had but one coolie wounded, but [it] is supposed [we] did the Enemy considerable damage. This day likewise a shot from the Enemy shattered a black boy's head to pieces near the house of Mr. Pindar, they still continuing throwing the stones one whereof lit in the Moody's Battery but did no damage; another upon the Great House in the Fort and made a hole quite through into the Long Room and beat the dust and stones upon the Company's table, but the stone came not through.

November 3, 1689

This day the Enemy fired several great guns and flung several stones at us, one whereof lit at the Judge's house just before the Fort Gate and killed one of my Lady's women.[94] They likewise flung a shell that broke near Ensign FitzGerald's house that is upon the Green which (praised be God) did no hurt.

November 4, 1689

The Enemy this day flung several stones at us, two whereof lit in the Fort, one on the curtain that goes from York Bastion[95] to the Company's Bastion and the other upon the Great House within a yard of the former, but did no hurt.

November 5, 1689

In the morning the Enemy flung four stones, none whereof lit in the Fort, and about noon they fired a shot which struck the Gate and broke the cross plate thereof but did no further damage. This day likewise one Edward Watterson, belonging to the 2d Company, ran away.

November 6, 1689

This day the Enemy came down as low as the hospital (being a parcel of new men lately come to the Sidi [who] were sent to try their valor) and

---

[94] "My Lady" was Susannah Child, née Shaxton, the wife of the governor. The woman who was killed would have been one of her servants or slaves.
[95] The location of this bastion is unclear.

our black people went out and fought them. About 3 o-clock in the afternoon his Excellency ordered out Lieutenant Bryan Carney with a party of men who engaged the Enemy and drove them from a new battery that they had behind Mr. Harris's house at the foot of Mount Whoredom[96] and in the pursuit of the Enemy our people saw several arms [i.e., weapons] lying on the ground. There was but one of our black people killed and four wounded, three whereof were English but not mortal. But it is thought by all that we have done them considerable damage, there being three heads and one silver mainlah[97] brought in to his Excellency. About 7 at night the Enemy likewise flung four stones, none whereof lit in the Fort neither did they any damage. His Excellency being informed that several of the Enemy's gallevats were to come in this night, sent an order off to all the Europe commanders to keep good looking out and have their boats ready upon occasion.

November 7, 1689

This evening was held a Court Martial for the trial of four of the Enemy's people who were taken as spies, but they could hardly be brought to confess anything but at last being urged to it, they confessed they were sent by the Sidi to view our fortification and strength of men, but could not be brought to confess anything further. Therefore it being late the Court was adjourned until another time. Between the hours of 8 and 12 in the evening the Enemy threw several stones, they flying over the Fort and (praised be God) did no damage.

November 8, 1689

This evening arrived here the Caesar, Captain Wright, the Betty, and the grab from Persia who brought several letters with them, likewise the Ruby Frigate, Captain Carr from the Northward and the Diana, Captain Charles Masters from Mahim who is now bound down the Coast for Calicut. About 10 o-clock at night the Enemy flung four stones at us, all of which flew over the Fort and did no damage.

November 9, 1689

This day the Enemy hath fired several shot at us, as likewise we at him, and between the hours of 9 and 12 in the evening the Enemy flung sev-

---

[96] The location of this obviously colloquial place name is unclear.
[97] Although the spelling is unusual, "mainlah" most likely refers to a manilha, that is, a bracelet or armlet.

eral stones at us, but (praised be God) we have received no damage and are uncertain what we may have done the Enemy.

November 10, 1689

The Enemy this evening likewise threw several stones at us, one whereof lit upon the bridge of a gun and broke it, which was on the curtain that goes from Caesar's Bastion to the Prince's Bastion but did no further damage.

November 11, 1689

About 9 o-clock at night we fired two bombs from the Fort but the Enemy hath not flung any stones this day. About 9 o-clock at night we fired two bombs at the Enemy and at 10 the Enemy flung four stones, none whereof lit in the Fort, neither did they any damage. This day likewise Thomas Crandill, William Cooley and James Potter, grenadiers, walking out behind the Company's Garden to see the Sidi's battery which is raised thereabout, they saw a man come out of the Sidi's battery in Moor's habit[98] and cried out to them in broken English: "Come here, come here." Then [this man] going in again [there] came out one Joseph Shaw (as they suppose, being known by his speech) who was formerly a grenadier and cried out to them "What cheer boys, come here, come here boys," upon which William Cooley fired at him and he at Cooley again. Then two great guns was fired out of the battery; all this time they saw this Shaw peeping out and in behind a bank and [he] fired at them two or three times.

November 13, 1689

This day one Charles Stacy belonging to the 3d Company ran away. At night we flung two shells at the Enemy; they presently after flung several stones at us but did no damage.

November 14, 1689

The Enemy as usual flung several stones at us but did no hurt.

---

[98] Meaning the standard dress of the Sidi army.

November 15, 1689

This day one Edward Robinson belonging to the 4th Company ran away; the Enemy at night still continuing flinging their stones.

November 16, 1689

The Enemy this day fired several shot at us, one whereof hit against the Company's Bastion and afterwards killed a black fellow that stood near Mitchell George's house. And at night they flung several stones which (praised be God) did no damage. This day likewise one of the washermen, being washing clothes at the tank, there came a great shot from the Enemy and shot him in the back and came out of his breast so that he immediately died.

November 17, 1689

This day the Enemy still continuing firing at us, one of the shot struck one of the stones that lay upon the wall on the Prince's Bastion and wounded one of the slaves in the leg. And between the hours of 6 and 7 at night the Enemy flung four stones, one whereof fell in the 3d Company's Guard and staved [in] a chest, but did no further damage, there being at that time several men lying upon the cots. This day likewise the Swede that fired the mortars being sick his Excellency sent off to Captain Wright to send one ashore if he had anyone that understood the firing of them.

November 18, 1689

This morning according to his Excellency's order Captain Wright sent his gunner ashore. This morning likewise the guns fired every half hour by his Excellency's order and about 5 in the evening we fired a shell at the Enemy which is supposed did them considerable damage. And about 7 the Enemy fired their stones as usual but did no harm. This day Mr. Cornwall, Captain Barber and Captain Utworth going out into the woods there came a great shot from the Enemy and shot off the arm of one John Croker belonging to Captain Barber as he was loading the said Captain Barber's piece.

November 20, 1689

John Gaudeen [a] soldier of the 2d Company ran away to the Sidi and about 10 this evening the Enemy flung his stones but did no damage.

November 21, 1689

This day we fired two shells at the Enemy, one whereof is supposed might do them damage but the other fell short, and about 9 in the evening the Enemy flung several stones but did no hurt.

November 22, 1689

This day Mr. Barker Hibbins and Mr. Staines went on the Ruby with a letter from his Excellency to the Governor of Surat.[99] This afternoon we flung two shells which is supposed did them damage and about 10 in the evening the Enemy flung several stones none whereof lit in the Fort nor did any hurt.

November 23, 1689

This day one Tom O'Neill of the 3d Company but belonging to the Hunter [Frigate] deserted the Garrison. We likewise flung two shells at the Enemy which is supposed might do them damage and between the hours of 11 and 12 at night the Enemy flung several stones which (praised be God) did no damage.

November 25, 1689

This day the Enemy fired several shot at us, one whereof lit on the end of the Long Room and beat down a great beam which fell amongst several black tailors that were then working there but did no hurt. This afternoon likewise we fired two bombs, one between the hours of 4 and 5 and the other between the hours of 5 and 6, both of which fell between Lieutenant Nangle's house and the Sessions House and is supposed might do the Enemy damage. This day one John Yates of the 1st Company and belonging to Sergeant Giles' guard-boat ran away.

November 27, 1689

This morning a shot from the Enemy killed a black woman lying upon her cot in her house upon the Green. About 3 in the afternoon we fired a shell at the Enemy which fell near Lieutenant Nangle's house.

---

[99] These were overtures for peace.

November 28, 1689

The Enemy fired several shot at us, one whereof hit the wall of the Great House and came through and broke a chair and beat the dust about the table where the Company's servants dine. Likewise [the Enemy] flung several stones at us, two whereof hit in the Fort but did no hurt. We likewise flung a shell at him which fell near the Sessions House and is supposed might do damage.

November 29, 1689

About one o-clock at night three men ran away from the [ship] Adventure with the [ship's] boat vizt: Edward Stubbs, Richard Gill and Robert Lightfoot, Captain Barber's servant, and carried with them a great quantity of gobbers,[100] some gold and plate, battery pistols, firelocks, swords [and sundry other] arms. His Excellency hath sent after them as low as Chaul and likewise wrote the Governor of Goa[101] and our friends at Karwar to secure them [i.e., arrest them] if they come that way.

November 30, 1689

This morning was seen a blazing star pointing from the East to the West over Karanja Point.[102] The Enemy hath flung several stones at us one whereof fell by Mr. Cooke's chamber (but praised be God) do no hurt. They likewise fired their great guns very briskly at us and we at them all this day, and in the afternoon were killed three black persons, a man, woman and boy.

December 1, 1689

This day the Enemy flung several stones at us but have done no damage thereby and likewise hath fired several great shot at us, some whereof hit the Great House. And about noon the Enemy fired a shot at us upwards of thirty pounds which took away a great piece out of the Fort Gate and wounded three or four Topasses setting in the Gateway.

---

[100] A gobber, possibly from Persian gabr, was a gold coin or ducat, likely denoting European origin. It was near in price to and often paired with a Venetian ducat, and in this period worth about 4 rupees.

[101] Goa was one of the oldest (from 1510) and largest Portuguese settlements in India. It is located about halfway down the west coast of India. Governor Child likely thought that the men would turn pirate.

[102] Meteors and comets were often at the time believed to be portents, usually of bad news.

December 2, 1689

This day the Enemy fired several shot and flung several stones at us and about noon one of the Enemy's great shot took off the leg of a child as it was picking up sticks near the house of Ensign FitzGerald on the Green but did no further damage. And about 4 in the afternoon we flung a shell at the Enemy which fell in the Enemy's battery at Lieutenant Nangle's house and is supposed might do them considerable damage.

December 3, 1689

This day the Enemy threw several stones and fired several shot at us some whereof hit the Great House in the Fort but did no further damage. And about 3 in the afternoon we threw a shell at the Enemy which broke outside Nangle's house and about 9 at night another which broke on the other side.

December 4, 1689

This day the Enemy flung several stones and fired several shot some whereof hit this house, but did no hurt.

December 5, 1689

This day the Enemy fired several shots and flung several stones but (praised be God) have done us no damage.

December 6, 1689

This morning the Enemy flung several stones at us which did no hurt and likewise fired several shot at us, some of which hit the Great House in the Fort and about 7 o-clock in the morning one of the shot lit in a room where several black tailors were a-working and shot one of them through the thigh. And about half past 7 a shot grazing upon the Green afterwards mounted [i.e., bounced] and fell upon the head of one John English, Sergeant of the 2d Company, as he was walking by his cotside upon the Prince's Bastion [and] being somewhat indisposed by the fall of which shot he immediately [died]. And between the hours of 5 and 6 in the evening we fired a bomb at the Enemy which fell near Judge Gary's house and is supposed might do them damage.

December 9, 1689

This day the Enemy fired several shot, one whereof hit against the Gateway but did no hurt.

December 11, 1689

Sergeant Kew came from Tannah[103] and brought with him Mahmud Zaid Beg[104] and tell us that one William Holland, soldier of the 3d Company, ran away out of his gallevat.

December 12, 1689

Ensign John Wyatt in the manchua with two gallevats went to Mahim to endeavor to take some of the Sidi's vessels which we had news appeared off from Mahim in the river.

December 13, 1689

About 4 o-clock in the afternoon his Excellency with his Guard of Grenadiers went on board the yacht and as his Excellency was going into the boat a great shot from the Enemy hit the stern of the Hopewell which lies ashore near the place where his Excellency took water [i.e., embarked] but (praised be God) did no mischief and about 5 was brought in a Coffree[105] for shooting his cabo [i.e., corporal] or commander through the hand and thigh at Sombooe's Battery who was committed to prison.

December 14, 1689

This morning was called a Court Martial for the trial of the Coffree that was committed to prison yesterday for shooting his cabo, and there appearing four witnesses against him who declared that he willfully shot the said cabo and would afterwards have made his escape. The prisoner having little to say for himself but that he was drunk, the Court gave judgment that for shooting his cabo and afterwards attempting to run away from his colors he deserved death, and so gave sentence as followeth, vizt. that he should be carried to the place from whence he came and there remain until Monday [the] 16th between 8 and 9 o-clock and from thence to be carried to Sombooe's Battery, where he committed

---

[103] Tannah (today, Thane) was the principal town on Salsette Island.

[104] A prominent and wealthy Surat merchant, whom Company officials regarded as a friend and an ally.

[105] The sources do not tell us whether this "Coffree" (African) was free or a slave. Some slaves were used as soldiers, but there seem to have been free people of African descent in Bombay town as well. Compare the outcome with a similar set of events on June 6–7, 1690.

this act, and there to be hanged by the neck until his body be dead dead dead.

December 16, 1689

Yesterday several shot passed between the Enemy and us [illegible] stones from the Enemy, but we received no damage from them and are unsure what they may have received from us. This morning the Coffree that shot his cabo on the 13th instant was hanged at Sombooe's Battery (being the place where he committed the act) according to sentence passed the 14th instant, the Enemy at the same time firing several shot at us and we at him. And about 5 in the afternoon the Enemy flung two stones one whereof lit on the Prince's Bastion and the other near the place where the first Company are quartered and cut off the leg of one Thomas Rodrigues belonging to the 4th Company and bruised his thigh so that he immediately died. And about 6 we fired two bombs, one whereof fell between the Moody's Battery and Lieutenant Nangle's house, at the breaking of which the top of it flew back into the Fort and fell near the Prison House and the other fell between Lieutenant Nangle's house and the Sessions House.

This night the long boats and barges of the Europe ships going out as usual to the Hunter Frigate that lieth near Cross Island, and there to cruise about to hinder all boats either from going in or coming out of Mazagaon, the Kempthorne's barge meeting with a canoe wherein was eight men and six of them rowers that put them hard to it to come up with them. But they in the barge continued firing and killed two of them, which discouraged the others so that they leapt all overboard, but were taken up by the barge's crew together with a packet of letters that was going to the Sidi which they had flung overboard. They had nothing in the boat but four great iron shot, one sword and four axes.

December 17, 1689

This day hath passed several shot between the Enemy and us and about 8 o-clock in the evening we fired a bomb at the Enemy which fell near Lieutenant Nangle's house and is supposed might do them damage. And about 11 the Enemy threw two Stones, one whereof lit in the middle of the place where the First Company are quartered and fell upon one end of a man's cot as he was lying thereon, but he suddenly starting up received no further damage than a bruise in his back. But the splinters of the said cot cut another man in the forehead to the skull, and the stone, after its fall, rebounded and flew over sixteen or eighteen men's cots and forced itself out at one end of the room but (praised be God) did no further damage.

December 18, 1689

This day the Enemy hath fired several shot at us and likewise threw several stones but did us no damage, and about 9 o-clock in the evening we fired a bomb at the Enemy which is supposed might do them damage. This day likewise Sergeant Lashly, coming from Mahim, met with two Dutch ships that came from Batavia[106] and [are] bound for Surat, and he going on board the admiral [i.e., the lead ship] they enquired what news between the Moors and us, and asked whether we wanted provisions. And they said that a ship directly from Holland that arrived Batavia before they came thence brought news that the Prince of Orange was crowned King of England on St George his day last past, and that King James was in Ireland and that the French had wars with all Europe Nations and with the Turk.[107] And they further said that they met with the Diana and the Sapphire, Captain Iver, bound from Madras[108] to the port of Bombay and that we may expect her here in a few days.

December 21, 1689

From the 18th instant to this day the Enemy hath flung several stones at us some whereof fell into the Fort, and likewise fired several great guns at us and we at them, but (praised be God) we have received no damage and are uncertain what the Enemy may have received. This day one John Stevens, formerly belonging to the yacht and now was taken [i.e., captured] in the gallevat belonging to the yacht, made his escape from the Enemy and came to us.[109] This day likewise one Hugh Lewis belonging to the 2d Company ran away.

December 22, 1689

This day the Enemy hath flung several stones at us, two or three of which fell in the Fort but (praised be God) did no damage. This evening

---

[106] Batavia (today, Jakarta) was, in the seventeenth century, the headquarters for Dutch East India Company (VOC) operations in Asia.

[107] William and Mary were crowned on April 11, 1689, which means the news took about eight months to reach the besieged fort. "The Turk" meant the Ottoman Empire.

[108] In the seventeenth century, Madras, also known as Fort St. George (today, Chennai), was the other major English East India Company fortified settlement located on the southeastern coast of what is now India.

[109] See Document 15.

we were alarmed by the Enemy by several volleys of shot that passed between him and our black soldiers without. The Enemy hath this night raised a new work at the pillory.

December 25, 1689

This day we fired a great many shells at the Enemy and several shot which made a breach at Nangle's House.

December 26, 1689

This day about 9 o-clock there came in the grenadiers' boat which gave us an account of the manchua and the rest of the boats which went in at Worli[110] and fought against the Enemy and sustained the damages as followeth: in the grenadiers' boat one William Gibbs mortally wounded by a great shot which took off his thigh close to his groin and John Shellcross wounded with a small shot in the wrist and one Topass killed belonging to the 4th Company. In Jackson's boat John Hewes, 4th Company, wounded in the tip of his shoulder and came out at his neck and one coolie shot through in the same boat. In Brookin's boat one coolie shot in the eyes. In Emett's boat one coolie wounded.

This day one William Osboldiston belonging to his Excellency's Guard of Grenadiers ran away to the Enemy. We have fired a great many guns and some shells at the Enemy's battery.

December 27, 1689

The Caesar set sail being bound down the Malabar Coast[111] there to take in pepper and from thence bound directly for England.

December 29, 1689

This day the Enemy hath fired a great many shot and flung several stones at us, but praised be God did us no damage.

December 30, 1689

This morning we received letters from Mr. Weldon and Mr. Navarro at [the Mughal] Court[112] wherein we find they are in great hopes of accommodation of peace.

---

[110] One of the islands and villages of the Bombay archipelago.
[111] The west coast of India.
[112] See Document 17.

January 3, 1690

From the 30th December to this day several shot have passed between the Enemy and us, but praised be God we have received no damage and are uncertain what the Enemy may have received. This evening the Enemy was very hot upon us (on sight of the new moon) with shots and stones, but we returned his salutes with several shot and one shell, which broke in the middle of Nangle's house and is supposed might do them great damage.

January 4, 1690

This day likewise one Mr. Oliver and Walter Galloway came to us from the Mughal's camp. This day the great gun that is at the new battery at Thorburn's house split.

January 5, 1690

About 5 o-clock in the evening arrived with us the Charles and John, Captain John Hunter, from Diu[113] who brought in with him a grab (laden with dates) as a prize, and at the same time arrived here the Sapphire Frigate, Captain Iver, from Madras with ammunition and provision and came [in] under his convoy the shybar that came down the coast with the Diana.

January 9, 1690

From the 5th instant to this day several shot have passed between the Enemy and us but praised be God we received no damage and are uncertain what the Enemy may have received. This day here a mortar piece that was at Thorburn's Battery split; there was another carried [in] in its room [i.e., in its place].

January 11, 1690

This evening we were alarmed by the Enemy by several volleys of shot that passed between them and our people without but received no damage.

---

[113] A Portuguese-controlled fortified port town at the entrance to the Bay of Cambay on the west coast of what is now India.

January 14, 1690

This afternoon we firing at each other a shot from the Enemy killed one Topass and took an English man's hand off belonging to the 2d Company on the Prince's Bastion.

January 15, 1690

About 9 o-clock at night the Enemy alarmed us and setting upon our out-sentries at Thorburn's Battery, but were repulsed by our people in the battery, they firing great guns from all their batteries round, and we likewise at them from the Fort, but (praised be God) we received no damage.

January 17, 1690

About 3 o-clock in the afternoon the Enemy made an attempt upon Thorburn's Battery but were repulsed by our Militia that lie there. A party of them being afterwards sent out by their Captain Michael George [they] killed two Englishmen[114] and one black and came off without receiving the least damage. We likewise fired a shell from the Fort that fell in the middle of Nangle's Battery and made a prodigious smoke and smother for a long time, and is supposed might do them considerable damage.

January 18, 1690

This afternoon Mr. Cornwall and Lieutenant Carney setting in the Gateway, the said Lieutenant being Captain of the Guard, a shot came against the gate, the splinters whereof wounded them both in the face, leg and left hand, and at the same time wounding the boy of the said Lieutenant Carney, but praised be God none of their wounds dangerous. And in the evening the Enemy flung several stones and some shells, two whereof not breaking were brought unto the Deputy Governor. But their shells and stones did us no damage.

January 19, 1690

One Leander Black belonging to the 3d Company ran away.

---

[114] These were presumably English deserters fighting on the side of the Sidi.

January 20, 1690

This morning one James Stevens, a montross, being about drawing of a gun, it being laden with partridge [shot], the gun evidently went off and shot off both his hands and bruised his head to pieces and likewise [so] mortified him in several other places that he immediately died.

January 21, 1690

This morning the Sidi flung one of our own shells (it being one of the largest) at us again which fell near the Fort Gate with the fuse downwards which broke off and bruised itself in the pile at the Fort Gate. Therefore praised be God [it] did no damage.

January 23, 1690

This day the Worcester Frigate, Captain Polsted, and the Charles and John, Captain Hunter, sailed out of the Road being both bound to the Northward.

January 26, 1690

This day the manchua and two gallevats went to Mahim River's mouth,[115] there to follow the orders of Captain Henry Benson in hindering the Enemy's boats going in or coming out there.

January 27, 1690

This evening the Enemy fixed several cannon baskets[116] at the dead wall at the mouth of the bazaar which is per computation within four yards of our battery at Thorburn's House.

January 28, 1690

This day two seamen belonging to the Kempthorne were brought in prisoners on suspicion of running to the Enemy.

---

[115] The body of water near the village of Mahim that separated Salsette from the Bombay archipelago.

[116] Cannon baskets (also called gabions) were fencelike structures, typically made of woven boughs and earth, used to protect the crews, cannon, and ordnance from incoming fire.

January 29, 1690

This evening, we having Information that the Enemies were at work, orders were given for firing each hour all night long, and about 12 at night John Mullins, the gunner's mate, fired a whole culverin on the Company's Bastion [and] it split in pieces and wounded him on the head, shoulders and several other places so that he immediately died. And a piece of the said gun wounded me in the face and cods [i.e., testicles] (so that they were forced to be sewn up) as I was sitting in the tent in the Fort yard and at the same time wounded Mr. Bathurst cutting him in the right side and bruising his back. This evening was taken near Sion by our ships' boats a boat belonging to a Moor with a boy and about three morahs of batty [i.e., rice] in her, the men all leaping overboard swam ashore and the boy declareth that they were going with the batty to the Sidi.

January 30, 1690

This day I went on board the hospital ship to get cured of my wounds I received on the 29th instant, it being more convenient than ashore.

February 1, 1690

About 12 at noon three [Enemy] boats putting off of Mazagaon, the Hunter Frigate fired a gun and gave notice thereof to the fleet, so that the ships' boats went up immediately, which they perceiving tacked about and made the best of their way for Mazagaon again. So that by the time our foremost ship's boat came within musket shot of them as they were under Mazagaon Fort the Sidi likewise manned out several other boats. Our boats [were] lying upon their oars [and] at the same time firing at the Enemy but finding that they would not come out and engage them returned again (praised be God) without any damage.

February 2, 1690

This day was taken in a Tannah[117] passage boat a stone cutter that used to cut [the] Enemy's stones that he fired at us and [who] formerly ran away from us. Last night the enemy raised up a work of palmares within

---

[117] Tannah, the principal town of Salsette Island, was also the name of the adjoining salt creek.

15 or 20 yards of Thorburn's Battery. This evening came a pattamar[118] that brought letters from Surat wherein was enclosed a proclamation proclaiming William and Mary, Prince and Princess of Orange, King and Queen of England, France and Ireland with the territories thereunto belonging.

February 3, 1690

This morning one Jasper Hampton belonging to the 3d Company, being at Thorburn's Battery, was shot through the body so that he lies dangerously ill, and in the afternoon they fired a shot from the said Thorburn's Battery which visibly did great execution. This day likewise Captain Kempthorne's two men that were put prisoners on the Guard the 28th January [are] now cleared.

February 4, 1690

This morning between the hours of 5 and 6 o-clock his Excellency Sir John Child departed this life and was buried from aboard the ship Blessing, the long boats and pinnaces, well-manned, attending him ashore where they fired three volleys. The Fort taking it from them fired small arms likewise, and so all the murchas[119] round about, and then the Fort fired forty-six guns [and] the ships taking it from the Fort fired in their stations.

February 8, 1690

This evening one of the shells broke upon the Prince's Bastion and flew about the Fort but praised be God did no damage (it was occasioned by the fuse being split). This day likewise a stone fell into Ensign FitzGerald's house and broke his table in pieces but did no further damage. This day orders were sent to Captain Ethrington to come into the Road being designed [to sail] down the Coast.

February 9, 1690

This day the Sapphire Frigate, Captain Iver Commander, sailed out of the Road being bound for Surat river's mouth.

---

[118] A courier, sometimes referring to a person and sometimes to a small coastal mail boat.
[119] An entrenchment or parapet (from Persian). Hilton uses it to mean a battery.

February 11, 1690

This morning the grab Friendship, Captain Teach Commander, sailed out of the Road being bound down the Coast, and in the afternoon passed by the Portuguese Armada. This day I came from aboard the hospital ship being pretty well recovered of my wounds I received the 29th January.

February 12, 1690

This evening we fired two bombs at the Enemy one whereof fell near Judge Gary's house, the other near the Portuguese Church, both [of] which broke well and is supposed might do the Enemy damage. The Enemy likewise flung several stones and fired several great guns at us, we firing also at him again as we hourly do, but we received no damage from the Enemy and are uncertain what we may have done him.

February 13, 1690

This morning the Enemy flung several stones at us, one whereof fell in Ensign FitzGerald's house (in the Fort) and broke down one side of the cot where he and his wife were lying, but (praised be God) did no damage. This day several shells were fired at the Enemy from Thorburn's Battery which we supposed might do execution.

February 14, 1690

This day Rama Comotin, shroff,[120] was wounded in the leg by one of our shells which broke as soon as fired out of the mortar.

February 15, 1690

This day a random shot from the Enemy fell in the grenadiers' boat and killed two of the grenadiers, namely Jack Pottes and Richard Dawson.

February 19, 1690

This day Robert Symonds who formerly was taken in the gallevat belonging to the yacht, being at an anchor about Cross Island, run away from the Enemy's lower battery, who declareth that the Sidi constantly lies at the Portuguese Church, and that he has not above five or

---

[120] A shroff was a merchant, banker, and money-changer (from the Persian or Arabic ṣarrāf).

six barrels of powder but daily expects more from Surat. He likewise declared many other things that are too tedious [i.e., time-consuming] here to insert. This afternoon a shot from the Enemy split one of the largest guns they had at Thorburn's Battery. This evening likewise the Enemy have raised a new work [defensive structure] at the Brahmanys' house being within half [a] pistol shot of Thorburn's Battery.

February 22, 1690

This day the Sidis advancing out of the battery, Ensign James, who hath been at Thorburn's Battery (ever since Michael George [went] to the other side[121] for his health being extreme ill), went out and fought them and advanced so far as to cut their cannon baskets. We received but little damage having but two black men killed, but are informed the Enemy had forty men killed besides wounded. This night we had two Englishmen run away to the Sidi belonging to the 3d Company, vizt: Nague Cheshire and John Bonnuck.

February 23, 1690

This afternoon came the manchua from Mahim so disabled by age that she could not swim [i.e., float] and gives an account of two grenadiers that ran from the boat, vizt: Richard Warren and Ruben More. The first had ran to the Sidi formerly and came back again. And here arrived a sloop from Surat with two Moor men of quality[122] one Mir Hossun and the other Hosson Chellaby[123] who brought letters from Mr. Weldon and Mr. Navarro with news of peace.

February 24, 1690

This morning went Mir Hossun and Hosson Chellaby to the Sidi with a flag of truce, and upon their return desired the Governor not to fire at the Enemy, for they would not fire at us desiring a cessation of arms.

February 25, 1690

This afternoon the Governor had news that the Enemy was at work [on their entrenchments] notwithstanding their word to the contrary, upon

---

[121] This probably means that Michael George went to the mainland, not that he deserted to the enemy.

[122] "Men of quality" means prominent and influential people; here, two very rich Surat merchants.

[123] Hossan Chellaby was a prominent merchant in Surat, whose family would continue to be involved in Bombay trade and politics into the eighteenth century.

which the Governor ordered the mortars to be laden and the guns to be laid at the Enemy. But upon request of Mir Hossun who wrote away to the Sidi, and at the Enemy's forbearance of working [i.e., stopping work], we did not fire.

February 26, 1690

At 12 o-clock at noon the Enemy having warning if they did any sort of work we should fire at them, Ensign James seeing them at work fired at them from his battery, so broke this cessation. The firing on both sides continued most of this afternoon; we fired several shells into their battery, which could not choose but [i.e, could not fail to] destroy a great many of their men.

February 27, 1690

This afternoon Ensign James came to the Fort and gave account that he suspected the Enemy's undermining of him. We were only sensible of their trenches not being above twenty yards from him [so] he might be very much in the right of it. So that he took two drums with him to try but no symptoms as we could find.[124] This day he hath dug a trench within his utmost palmares about eight yards [long] with a design to set up palmares there [so that] in case the Enemy should spring up a mine[125] he would have a retreat, and within his works [he] hath planted two great guns. Last night the Enemy flung two iron shells into his battery which killed two black men. The Enemy hath had fifteen great guns within thirty-five or forty yards of this battery of ours these three weeks but (praised be God) hath done little harm to us. The Enemy likewise split one of our great guns. The Enemy continued heaving of stones which we formerly gave an account of, but take little or no notice of them by reason they do us no damage.

February 28, 1690

This morning the Worshipful John Vauxe, Deputy Governor, ordered all the men to be drawn up and had his commission read and delivered the same to Mr. George Cooke and left him the government of the place [illegible] he [Vauxe] being forced to go to Surat to receive

---

[124] Presumably he was using the drums to search for echoes or vibrations that would suggest tunneling on the part of the enemy.

[125] A mine was a tunnel. To "spring up a mine" was to tunnel under the enemy's defenses and then try to blow them up from beneath.

the Mughal [emperor]'s farman,[126] it being the [emperor's] desire he should receive it and none else. And [he] took Mr. Cornwall [as] secretary with him. He likewise took with him twelve Englishmen and one servant, and embarked about 3 this afternoon on the Royal James and Mary. The Moor general that came from Surat returned back with him and when he left from the shore Mr. Cooke gave him twenty guns and fired them all towards the Enemy. This day the Enemy disabled two of our guns at the batteries.

March 2, 1690

Being the first sight of the new moon the Enemy fired very smartly at us and we at him.

March 3, 1690

Mr. Cooke ordered two whole culverins to be brought to the Prince's Bastion to ply at the Enemy's battery that they have at the head of the bazaar and ordered Michael George with his men to go to a new battery we have built at Mr. Harris's house which is between the church and Thorburn's Battery, and ordered some new Topasses that came over to go in their room to Ensign James at Thorburn's Battery. This afternoon about two o-clock the Enemy's battery took fire by a shell Ensign James fired into it from his battery, and he did so ply them with shells and guns that they could not put it out. This battery of the Enemy's is within forty yards of ours, formerly called the Brahmanys' house, being a great large house. Captain Iver arrived from Surat in the Sapphire Frigate who brought letters from Mr. Weldon and Mr. Navarro, likewise from the Agent and General at Surat,[127] the which gave an account of a certain [i.e., confirmed] peace that the Mughal had granted to us. The Enemy's battery continued firing until 9 this night.

March 4, 1690

This afternoon the Enemy's battery sprung up a fresh fire until 11 at night; we were in hopes it would have run on the whole line that the Enemy hath against our battery, which consisteth of the fifteen great guns before mentioned. But the wind being contrary did not prove so.

---

[126] A farman (from the Persian farmūdan, "to command") was an imperial grant or order from the Mughal emperor (see Document 18).

[127] Bartholomew Harris, the president of the Surat factory.

March 5, 1690

This night Mr. Cooke ordered two saker guns[128] in the room of two minions[129] that they had at the Moody's Battery, by the reason of the scarceness of our minion shot. Likewise this night our black soldiers has put up a work[130] from Ensign James's [Battery] to that of Captain George's, which is in order of making a line of communication from one to the other. This night likewise fell upon the Caesar's Bastion a large round stone cut hollow and filled up with brimstone and powder which the Enemy flung out of their mortar in the imitation of a shell, with a fuse, but it did no damage, being not capable thereof unless it fell amongst some cadjan combustible stuff. The Enemy hath fired several of them but we took no notice thereof before this by reason none of them ever fell in the Fort.

March 6, 1690

This day the Enemy has fired briskly at us and likewise flung several stones, some whereof fell in the Fort but did no damage. But about 11 o-clock in the evening a shot from the Enemy hit against part of the curtain that goes from the Prince's Bastion to Caesar's Bastion and killed one Benjamin Martin, Sergeant of the 2d Company.

March 8, 1690

This morning about 4 or 5 o-clock Ensign James went out to set upon the Enemy's trench that is between their and our battery, and went up to it and fired his pistol into it and set afire the cotton bags that were at the head of the trench and cut their cannon baskets, and killed several of the Enemy as they lay in the trench, upon which the Enemy sallied out, and made a hot engagement. On our side the damage being but little, having one English dangerously wounded and three blacks killed outright, with about fourteen blacks wounded, we were forced to leave one of our Christian fellows' body behind. The Enemy by all computation cannot have lost less than sixty or seventy men having four dead bodies [left] behind. This night about 9 or 10 o-clock the Enemy came up near Ensign James's battery to desire leave of carrying off their dead bodies upon which he told them if they would come in the daytime with a flag of truce they might have them. They said if we would let them carry off

---

[128] Medium-sized cannon.
[129] Fairly small cannon (the manuscript is hard to decipher here).
[130] Presumably a trench.

their dead we should have our dead body, but Ensign James told them he knew of none he had there but if he had any he did not much value them. They not agreeing in their discourse he bid them be gone, which they not obeying he fired a gun with partridge [shot] in amongst them which made them retire to their own murcha.

March 9, 1690

About 7 o-clock this evening Ensign James, seeing some of the Enemy, fired some shot, one of which killed the English drummer belonging to the 2d Company [and] wounded two more.

March 10, 1690

This morning about 2 o-clock the Enemy being provided with ladders, fire pots and bottles full of powder, came along the sand side up almost as high as Nicholl's Folly[131] and so came down the back side of the Company's garden, as we found by their track afterwards. The sentry that was without the works, being careless of any that should come behind him, [was] looking continually towards the Enemy's battery and that way heard a great noise behind him and turning about asked who they were and discharged his musket, upon which they rushed in upon him and cut him in the hand and wrung his musket from him, upon which he took to his heels and run without giving any further alarm to the battery. The Enemy kept on their full speed until they got under our battery and there set up their ladders and entered in a little work just without [the] battery door, being computed to be about three hundred of them. Our subadar, being Maloji Bhonsle[132] by name, being surprised at his men's weak-heartedness in letting the men come in, cried out "Will you quit the battery and so be hanged by the English? It is better for you to fight like men," which words got some of them about him and he himself with the Christian cabo maintained the door and killed about twenty of the Enemy.

The Enemy continued throwing in their bottles and pots of powder the which burned five of our men to a great degree. But at last one of the Enemy was known to Maloji Bhonsle by his voice to be his brother-

---

[131] Perhaps near the spot where Captain Nicholls and others attempted to board the Sidi's ship in 1683 (see Document 9).
[132] Maloji Bhonsle was a Maratha officer.

in-law (that was in the Sidi's service) who lanced him in the mouth so to the jaw bone but [we] are in great hopes he will recover again. But they at the door forced the Enemy to retreat into the fire which they themselves had made by setting the cadjan houses on fire that were within the little work. Mr. Cooke sending out of [i.e., for] ammunition by Dorab[133] and ordering him to get some [persons] to go for the succor of the battery, he took with him those men that belongs to Khanderi[134] that lay at Mr. Butler's house by the waterside, and upon their entering the garden with ammunition, and the day breaking out, the Enemy retreated. They attempted the entry of the battery in several places besides this part where the door stood, but our men beat them off.

When we went out to see what damage the Enemy had done we found three of their bodies, one lying in the fire (we formerly spoke of) and four ladders which two men might go up abreast, and found them all bloody. Likewise [on] the walls where they attempted the entry and all in the fields near about the battery [were] found a great many lumps of blood which makes us conclude they must have lost a considerable number of men. According to the ground they took up when they assaulted our battery [we] cannot compute them to be less than three thousand. The loss that we sustained at this battery [was] not above twelve wounded and nine killed. This time the enemy was not idle with us on the other side of the Green, for they likewise fell upon the Moody's Battery, but lighting such a peel of partridge shot and small shot hindered them from their assault. One of the Enemy came just to the top of the palmares whose head was brought in to Mr. Cooke, and upon their being beaten off our men sallied out and found several bundles of cadjans to a great quantity as we supposed with a design to lay them under our palmares and so to burn our battery. We found here vast quantities of blood. In the time of engagement the enemy fired several great shot and so did we at them, and they fired two iron shells, the one of which broke over the Fort and the other just under the Fort wall. About 7 of the clock the officers of the murchas came and gave our Governor an account of what had happened and he returned them the praise due for so good an action and ordered that the Company's Garden murcha should have a couple of great guns.

---

[133] Dorab ("Drab" in the original) was most likely Rustom Dorabji, a Parsi trader and boat owner prominent in the Zoroastrian community at Bombay.

[134] Khanderi, or Kenery, was a tiny island in the bay that had been fortified by the Marathas. (Sidi Yakut, their archenemy, had fortified the only slightly larger neighboring island of Underi.)

March 11, 1690

This afternoon Mr. Cooke went out to visit the murchas and to order that they should not have any cadjan houses in the inner side of their batteries but have palmares instead of cadjans and cover the [roof] trees[135] with earth. And when he went into the Company's garden he called all the officers and soldiers together and made a short speech to them of their good behavior and gave them 1000 xeraphins in part of their pay, with encouragement [that] if they behaved themselves well they might expect the whole in a short time. And he likewise ordered that all those houses which lay under the Fort walls should be pulled down because they blinded some of our guns and likewise ordered Sir John Wyborn's house to be better fortified and ordered some more men and ordered them to make up [i.e., barricade] the windows of the old church with palmare trees.

March 14, 1690

This morning the Shrewsbury, Captain Richard Ethrington, came from Surat.

March 15, 1690

This afternoon the Shrewsbury set sail for Karwar and those two days last passed we have not been idle for we and the Enemy have fired a great many great [i.e., large] shot at each other and small arms every night.

March 17, 1690

This morning Mr. James Butler died.

March 18, 1690

This day about noon Captain William Iver sailed for Surat and Mr. Cooke ordered me for to make two powder chests for to lay under the church wall in case the Enemies assault there [so as] to blow [it] up.

March 19, 1690

This afternoon the black soldiers belonging to the Savajee mutinied for their pay and declared they would not serve any longer without it. And

---

[135] "Roof trees" is an old term for roof beams.

with our colors flying that the General gave them and trumpets sounding [they] marched towards the Old Woman's Island.[136] Mr. Cooke ordered me to get ten files of men ready to fetch them back, upon notice of which they came back of their own accord. All day yesterday and today the Enemy hath plied their shot very hot at us and this night shot one of our montrosses with a great shot in the thigh, William Garett by name.

March 20, 1690

This morning early Mr. Cooke sent for all the nayaks[137] to be brought to the Fort that were in the mutiny. This day we had one Thomas Smart, Corporal that belonged to the 2d Company, who was ordered with Ensign James at his battery, shot in the foot with a small shot.

March 21, 1690

This day we placed the two powder chests in the ground at the church and we had one Englishman wounded in Ensign James's Battery, namely Henry Hevland, montross. And Mr. Cooke, finding several of our people absent and killed that belonged to their former guard, ordered their quarters at the several bastions anew,[138] and ordered me to go out and muster the black soldiers in order to [receive] their payment. And about 7 or 8 o-clock at night the Enemy set upon the Moody's Battery and brought some cadjans with a design to lay them under the palmares as formerly but were beaten off by our small shot. They threw down their cadjans and set them afire themselves some distance from our battery, the light of which gave our men opportunity to fire their small shot at them and beat them off. And [between] about 11 and 12 this night they set up a great shout and run up to Ensign James's and the Moody Battery and fired their small arms at them but our people soon beat them over.

March 22, 1690

This day at noon Captain Carr in the Ruby and the Emerald, Captain Harrison, came into the Road from cruising to the Northward, the latter dying as he came in.

---

[136] Old Woman's Island was in fact two small islands (Colaba and Little Colaba, or Upper and Lower Colaba) at the south end of the archipelago, just below Bombay town and the Fort.

[137] Nayak (literally "leader," from Sanskrit) here probably refers generally to the commanders of the "black" soldiers mentioned in the previous entry.

[138] Reassigned people to the various bastions.

March 23, 1690

Mr. Cooke ordered Captain Prestwich who lies ashore to bring as many guns as he could to clear the hospital and tombs and ordered him a file of men for his assistance and likewise ordered my sergeant, John Wye, with three of the grenadiers, which were all we had ashore, to lie at the hospital to throw grenade shells in case of an assault.

March 24, 1690

This day our Enemy fired very much and about the hours of 9 and 10 at night fired two iron shells at our battery of which one part came into the middle of the Fort.

March 25, 1690

This day we had great firing. At night the Enemy fired five shells of which there was but one did not break, and continued firing their great guns all night.

March 26, 1690

This morning the Enemy began again firing their great guns very early and continued all day but did us no harm excepting one Englishman belonging to the First Company, namely Hugh Bowes.

March 27, 1690

About 4 or 5 in the evening the Enemy sprung their mine which they had against Ensign James's Battery but it broke backwards on them-selves, the which we believe might do them a great deal of harm, for their trenches were full of men that led to the mine. Ensign James had made a counter mine a little without [i.e., outside] his trench, of which the Enemy's mine broke but about a yard short. The enemy continued plying their great shot almost all this night. This evening the Little Cae-sar, Captain Whittle, came into the Road from China.

March 28, 1690

This day John Jessop died. The Enemy this day still continued plying their great shot at us.

March 30, 1690

This day came John Elsley in one of the guard-boats from Mahim who adviseth us that one John Barham being ran away from Emett's Boat. These two days last past the Enemy continued firing their great shot very smartly at us but did us no damage. This night about 8 or 9 o-clock there came a Moor man[139] and this morning about one o-clock the Enemy approached towards the hospital. But on their coming the Emerald Frigate that Mr. Cooke had ordered to lie there to clear the fore part of the hospital and Captain Prestwich's ship (that Mr. Cooke had ordered some men aboard) lay in the Bay plying some shot [so] the Enemy soon retreated. But at the same time some of them came down to our bazaar or marketplace and took some poor coolie women and children to the account [i.e., number] of twenty.

April 2, 1690

This day the Emerald, Mr. Dingle, Commander, sailed for Surat.

April 5, 1690

For these three days last past the Sidi hath fired but very few shot. This afternoon Ensign James came to Mr. Cooke and informed him the Enemy's mine was just come to his countermine, but something [i.e., somewhat] under it, and by the judgment of our miners not above five foot off, for he could hear them talk very plainly in their mine. So Mr. Cooke called all the Commission officers and asked their opinions and what was best to do. So they saying nothing he told them what I had proposed to do, which was to lay in the head of our countermine (for it was not above four foot broad and not above seven in depth) three great iron shells that held fourteen pound of powder each and to stop up the mine very close and so to fire them so to break into the Enemy's [mine] and disable them from working any further, the which was done out of hand. And Ensign James stopped it up so well and gave fire to it about 10 o-clock at night [so] that it all broke out of the Enemy's mouth of their trenches and fell in the matter [i.e., collapsed the sides] of 12 or 14 yards of the Enemy's mine, the which occasioned a great cry amongst the Enemy that our people heard them very plain.

---

[139] A ship owned by a Muslim merchant.

April 7, 1690

This day at noon Captain John Kempthorne sailed for Surat, and about 2 o-clock Ensign James's Battery took [i.e., caught] fire, the which occasioned the Enemy to fire very smartly. But Ensign James behaved himself so well that by sunset he got it out. Mr. Cooke ordered him a Sergeant and six files of men to strengthen his battery, by reason that that part of it was burned down where the fire took and [also] to keep the black people constantly throwing water [on it] all night long, for the enemy kept plying of their fire arrows out of their great guns to set it afire again. We had one Englishman wounded, Thomas Swetman, gunner of the said murcha and several black men killed and wounded.

April 9, 1690

This morning about 2 o-clock the Enemy came to the hospital towards the head of the bazaar, but those men that Mr. Cooke ordered [to lie] at Sir John Wyborn's house soon beat them away and they likewise sat upon all our murchas round who were soon beaten off. We sustained no loss of our side only one Peter Richards wounded at Ensign James's Battery and Henry Hevland.

April 10, 1690

This day about 10 o-clock the Sidi put out a white flag at the Mint House and Mr. Cooke ordered Lieutenant Magregory to meet the messenger who was Mir Horsum's[140] servant who came from Surat overland and gave an account of the Worshipful John Vauxe having received the Mughal's farman and that a gurzbardar[141] was a-coming in the Sapphire. [The messenger said] the Sidi desired a cessation and that his master was with the Sidi, and if Mr. Cooke gave leave [he] would come and wait upon him, which was granted, and about two hours afterwards he [Mir Horsum] came himself. And this day came the Sidi's steward, Mir [Nur] Mahmud and Mir Horsum to Mr. Cooke and Mr. Cooke desired that there might be articles of a cessation drawn up, the which he agreed to, but desired he would send a gentleman to visit the Sidi as he [the Sidi] had sent him to visit Mr. Cooke.[142]

---

[140] This may be the same person as Mir Hossun, who appears earlier in the diary.
    [141] A gurzbardar (Gozbardar in the original) was a Mughal messenger and macebearer, in this case sent for the ceremonial announcement of the terms of peace.
    [142] Honor required that the diplomacy go both ways.

April 12, 1690

This morning came Captain Carver in the Success laden with corn (for the Garrison) from the Northward. This afternoon myself and Mr. Thurscross were sent to visit the Sidi and to discourse him about the articles of a cessation, the which we carried with us drawn up by Mr. Cooke and were accordingly agreed to by the Sidi.

April 13, 1690

This day Pedro Fernando, a European belonging to the 3d Company, run away.

April 14, 1690

This day came Captain Iver from Surat and I went to the Sidi and carried him the articles in Persian in the which he made some small objection.

April 16, 1690

Captain Iver went for Surat and I went to the Sidi and he signed the articles.

April 23, 1690

About one o-clock Mr. Samuel Staines died.

April 25, 1690

This day the cessation being out the Sidi sent Nur Mahmud to let Mr. Cooke know he could not make war with us again until he had further orders from the King [i.e., the Mughal emperor] and the Governor of Surat being that our Governor Vauxe had received the King's farman and was settled at Surat, so it was agreed the cessation should last and that they that had a mind to break [it] should give 24 hours' warning first on either side.

April 28, 1690

This afternoon arrived one Captain Minchin from Madras in the ketch Samuel laden with ammunition and some provisions for us.

April 29, 1690

This day Captain Charles Masters came from Calicut.

May 1, 1690

This morning came the Emerald from Surat and a Moor's ship that was bound for Bengal.

May 2, 1690

This day the Ruby sailed for Surat laden with treasure.

May 3, 1690

This morning sailed the Emerald and yacht for Surat likewise laden with treasure.[143]

May 7, 1690

This day the prize ship Hossaune sailed for Surat.

May 12, 1690

Sergeant Stevenson arrived from Surat with six of his men who gave us advice of [i.e., let us know about] the gurzbardar's being set out of Surat.

May 15, 1690

This morning came Captain Iver in the Sapphire and Captain Beere in the Quedah Merchant from Surat, the first being bound for Madras the other for Acheen and Quedah,[144] and the Shrewsbury likewise arrived from the Coast.

May 16, 1690

This day the Emerald came from Surat; the Sapphire and Quedah Merchant sailed out of the Road. This day Ensign John Wyatt in one of our boats sent to Bassein for that purpose brought down the gurzbardar to Mazagaon.

May 17, 1690

This day I was sent by Mr. Cooke to compliment the gurzbardar, who the same day delivered [to] the Sidi the King's farman and order to depart the Island.

---

[143] This was presumably in part payment of the large fine demanded by the Mughal emperor to end the siege.

[144] Acheen and Quedah (today Aceh and Kedah) were two southeast Asian ports.

May 18, 1690

The gurzbardar came to the Fort and complimented Mr. Cooke, telling him he would not depart until the Sidi was gone off the Island, to further which he desired us (it being late in the year) to assist him with some of our boats, which we accordingly did. One Thomas Gattlett that run away the beginning of the war came [back] to us, he being cut[145] and William Cooley and Michael Bartlett, grenadiers, ran away from us.

May 23, 1690

From the 18th to this day there has been people passed between the Sidi and us,[146] and this day I went with a free pardon from Mr. Cooke into the Sidi camp, it being for all Englishmen as well them that were cut as them that were not. But none would come excepting one William Osboldiston that was formerly a grenadier, although they [that] were not turned Moors had the Sidi's grant to go or stay.[147] This evening Dorab's shybar went away laden with the Sidi's guns, and the sloop was ordered to Dongri to assist in carrying away the remainder and this day one John Green that was cut made his escape from the Sidi upon sight of the aforesaid pardon.

May 24, 1690

This morning about thirty or forty boats passed by fully laded with Moor baggage [and the like] and in three or four of them were Englishmen who impudently as they passed by the Fort called to our men, so suppose the Sidi has sent all or most of his Englishmen off the Island. This afternoon one John More and John Gaudeen, one of the 1st [and] the other of the 2d Company, that some time since deserted this Garrison, returned upon sight of the pardon, as likewise one Reuben More, formerly [a] grenadier. This day one John Hall of the 1st Company; Robert King and Jonathan Naked, 2d Company; John Oliver and Thomas Hutchings, 3d [Company]; John Young, 4th [Company]; and John Claudy, montross, deserted the Garrison.

---

[145] Circumcised as part of conversion to Islam.

[146] This was an exchange of prisoners of war.

[147] Once one had converted to the "true" religion, whatever it was, one was not typically free to change back again (this was also true in much of Christian Europe at the time). Hence, in theory the Sidi would not let go those who had actually converted to Islam. In practice those who wanted to return to Bombay seem to have had little trouble doing so.

May 25, 1690

This day the yacht Josiah, Captain Benjamin Stacy, Commander, came into the Road from Surat river's mouth.

May 28, 1690

Arrived here the Ship Benjamin, Captain Leonard Browne, Commander, having been eleven months from England and confirmed the news that King James was in Ireland and that William, Prince of Orange, and Mary, his Princess, were proclaimed King and Queen of England. She likewise brought from [the Island of] St Helena twenty-one men, women and children but no soldiers from England.[148]

June 2, 1690

This day the Sidi delivering up part of the Island the Worshipful George Cooke ordered me to go and take possession of the same and to place the following persons in their respective stations vizt: At the Portuguese Church: Ensign William James with Santsenay and his ranch[149] of Hindus— (174); [and] Domingo D'Silva and his Christians (59)

At Dongri Hill: Nogg Nayak with Bandareens— (100); Phillip Vass
    with Christians— (55)
At the Right Honorable Company's Warehouse: Ragogy Purpatraw (58)

All which were immediately drawn [up] upon the Green before the Moody's Battery and in the afternoon, having orders from the gurzbardar, marched into their several possessions, where I seated them with strict orders not to suffer any English, Hindus or others to pass the bounds of the precincts. And if any should presume to go further without leave from the Governor, to seize such offenders and bring them away prisoners to the Fort and likewise gave strict charge to the aforementioned commanders that they keep good watch and suffer none of the Sidi's people to come within our quarters or have any correspondence with them.

---

[148] St. Helena is a small island in the South Atlantic that was controlled and settled by the English East India Company. First obtained in 1658, and briefly occupied by the Dutch in 1673, the island was populated by settlers and their slaves and was used to water and provision the Company's ships on the return trip from Asia.

[149] The source of the term "ranch" is not clear, but it apparently means "company." In parentheses next to each commander is the number of men in the ranch or company.

June 6, 1690

This day a Court Martial was held on one Sergeant John Stevenson and Corporal Laughlin Flynn who, on the 21st past month, resisted the guard that was sent out to command all Englishmen into the Fort, and in their resistance wounded two men, one through the arm and thigh and the other through the arm, which action merited no less than death. But the Court out of compassion to their own countrymen ordered their punishments as followeth: that they should be the next day discharged from their former employs at the head of the four companies and to be kept in custody of the Provost Marshal until such time as a ship [was] ordered for England, and then to work their passage home, and during their imprisonments to be allowed no more than the Garrison provisions now established.

June 7, 1690

This day the aforesaid Sergeant John Stevenson and Corporal Laughlin Flynn were brought out into the Fort Parade at the head of the four Companies and there discharged of their former employs and then returned again to the prison by the Provost Marshal, as was yesterday by the Court Martial ordered.

June 9, 1690

This day arrived Mr. Abraham Navarro from Court, he having left Mr. Weldon at Surat and this day the gurzbardar came to the Fort.

June 19, 1690

Yesterday the gurzbardar sent an eddy[150] to acquaint us that we might take possession of Mahim, Sion and all other parts of the Island except Mazagaon, whereupon the Worshipful George Cooke marched out to the Portuguese Church with all our field forces and about 9 o-clock in the morning dispatched Lieutenant Bryan Carney for Mahim and Ensign William James for Sion with the following forces:

With Lieutenant Carney: Englishmen (24); Ramajee Anutt with his ranch of Hindus (138); Bonjee Pattel with his ranch of Hindus (42);

---

[150]An eddy (aḥadī) was a mid-level gentleman trooper or cavalryman, below a ranked nobleman (mansabdar); in this case, he is serving as an imperial messenger.

Jos Pererra with his ranch of Christians (51) [for a total of]
255 [men]
With Ensign James: Santsenay with his ranch of Hindus (174); Dom
D'Silva with his company of Christians — (59) [for a total of]
233 [men]

June 21, 1690

One Carly Makarly belonging to the 3d Company deserted the Garrison.

June 22, 1690

This morning the Sidi departing the Island with all his forces John
FitzGerald was ordered to march and take possession of Mazagaon
having with him the following forces: Garrison soldiers — (12); Xaviera
Gomes with Christians (51); Maloji Bhonsle with Hindus — (200) [for a
total of] 263 [men].

And this afternoon the Worshipful George Cooke ordered me to draw
out all the grenadiers and two Englishmen and one Topass out of each
Company to take possession of the Portuguese Church.

An account of what guns we had disabled during the time of these
wars:

*[The following entry lists guns split or disabled in the various batteries
and on the bastions but is left out for reasons of space.]*

A list of what men has been killed, wounded and what has ran away to
the Enemy from the beginning of the wars to the ending thereof:

*[In the interest of space, the wounded, many of whom subsequently died,
are not listed here. They consisted of some 131 people. As with the list of
the dead, most of the English bear proper names while most of the others
are listed generically (i.e., 4 Savajees, 1 slave, 30 blacks) (see Figure 2).*

*The names of the 115 men who "ran" (deserted) are also not listed
here, though many of them are mentioned by name in the body of the
diary itself. Judging by their names, about 67 (just over half) were
English or northern European and most of the remainder were Indo-
Portuguese or Portuguese with a few Frenchmen.]*

Killed (104)

Alexander Monroe, Ensign and	two or three men Killed
14 men more with ammunition	Lieutenant Nangle
one Bandareen	Sombooe
three soldiers	William Ardis
Captain Hubbard	Frognall
Ensign Browne	5 or 6 Blacks
Lewis d'Souza	1 English
1 coolie	30 Bandareens
Scales a grenadier	Dennis Gublin
1 man Captain Cooke's Boat's crew	2 Blacks
1 man belonging to the Shrewsbury	1 Black
1 man	1 washerman
Richard Finch	1 Black woman
William Sanders	1 man ⎫
Samuel, a boy	1 woman ⎬ Black
1 Man on board the battery ships	1 boy ⎭
2 Blacks	3 Topasses
2 Blacks	1 Topass
John Mulins	9 Blacks
James Patten ⎫	Wm Gibbs
Robert Dawson ⎭ by a great shot in their boat	Henry Arno

When the Enemy was quite gone off the Island that we could come to have a full view of all their works, we found a prodigious number of palmares set up on end and cannon baskets filled full of earth (at least four yards in the diameter) at all the batteries, which was their way of fortification. And we likewise found two great trenches that they had thrown up. One [went] from Lieutenant Nangle's house down to the mouth of the bazaar or market place, being by computation 200 yards in length and of measured breadth three yards and a half and in depth one yard and a half. The other went from behind the pillory down within 40 or 50 yards of our battery at the end of which was dug two mines both of an equal breadth and depth vizt: breadth: two yards and a half, and depth: two yards, and in length underground: 47 yards. This trench (they proceeded from) was about two yards in breadth and two and a half in depth in some places, by computation about 250 yards in length.

Figure 2. James Hilton, *Count of Dead and Wounded from the Diary*, 1690

This page from late in James Hilton's diary represents the final tally of wounded and dead after Sidi Yakut had finally left the island. Crosses next to the names of the wounded probably means they died of their wounds. Hilton provides no reckoning of those who died of the plague or other epidemic diseases, almost certainly a higher number than died from enemy action.

The British Library Board, IOR G/3/3 fol. 43 (Bombay Diary 1689–1690)

The aforesaid mine was dug underground within two or three yards of the trench of our battery, but our diligence in countermining did oppose them that they could proceed no further. They had in all seven batteries all [of] which was strongly built with those palmares and cannon baskets full of earth and guns in every one of them. They had likewise twenty-two guns that plied continually against Thorburn's Battery.

Perused July 26, 1695[151]

---

[151] This final notation marks the date when the diary was officially read by the Company leadership back in London. The reason for the long time-gap between when it was written and when it was read is unclear. Bombay appears to have sent the diary to London in February 1691.

PART THREE

Related Documents

1

The East India Company on the West Coast of India

1

JOHN OVINGTON

The Great Rival to Bombay: The Port of Surat and Indian Ocean Trade
1689

John Ovington, who served as a chaplain in the East India Company, visited Surat in 1689 and later published his impressions of the city, which is less than 200 miles to the north of Bombay. Surat was the principal Mughal seaport in western India, home to some of the empire's greatest merchants and the main embarkation point for Indian Muslims undertaking the hajj, or pilgrimage to Mecca. Since 1616, the East India Company had maintained a "factory" (that is, a residence and trading house) in Surat, from which it directed all of its operations in western India, Persia, and Arabia. By the 1680s, Company leaders began to try to turn their colony of Bombay into a rival to Surat, though at this point the island was still quite small and in many respects still very dependent on and connected to the Surat trade. Ovington's account pays a good deal of attention to the mechanics of trade, but it is also full of detail about social and cultural practices, especially among the Europeans resident in the city.

John Ovington, *A Voyage to Suratt in the Year 1689* (London: Jacob Tonson, 1696), 218–19, 221–22, 279–80, 282, 385, 391–92, 394–401, 405, 408–9.

Surat is reckoned the most famed emporium of the Indian Empire, where all commodities are vendible, though they never were there seen before. The very curiosity of them will engage the expectation of the purchaser to sell them again with some advantage, and will be apt to invite some other by their novelty, as they did him, to venture upon them. And the river is very commodious for the importation of foreign goods, which are brought up to the city in hoys and yachts and country boats, with great convenience and expedition. And not only from Europe, but from China, Persia, Arabia, and other remote parts of India, ships unload abundance of all kinds of goods, for the ornament of the city, as well as [the] enriching of the port.

It is renowned for traffic through all Asia, both for rich silks, such as atlasses, cuttanees, sooseys, culgars, allajars, velvets, taffeties, and satins; and for zarbatss[1] from Persia; and the abundance of pearls that are brought hither from the Persian Gulf; but likewise for diamonds, rubies, sapphires, topazes, and other stones of splendor and esteem, which are vendible here in great quantities; and for agates, cornelians, nigganees,[2] desks, scrutores [i.e., portable writing desks] and boxes neatly polished and embellished, which may be purchased here at very reasonable rates. . . .

The Indians are in many things of matchless ingenuity in their several employments and admirable mimics of whatever they affect to copy after. The Banian, by the strength of his brain only, will sum up his accounts with equal exactness, and quicker dispatch, than the readiest arithmetician can with his pen. The weavers of silk will exactly imitate the nicest and most beautiful patterns that are brought from Europe. And the very ship-carpenters at Surat will take the model of any English vessel, in all the curiosity [i.e., complexity] of its building, and the most artificial [i.e., inventive] instances of workmanship about it, whether they are proper for the convenience of burthen or of quick sailing, as exactly as if they had been the first contrivers [i.e., inventors]. The wood with which they build their ships would be very proper for our men of war [ships] in Europe for it has this excellence that it never splinters by the force of a bullet, nor is injured by those violent impressions beyond the just bore of the shot. The tailors here fashion the clothes for the Europeans, either men or women, according to every mode that

---

[1] These are all varieties of cloth, most of them luxury cloth.
[2] Nigganee (Niccanee or Nickanee) was a sort of inexpensive striped calico.

prevails; and fit up the commodes[3] and towering head-dresses for the women, with as much skill, as if they had been an Indian fashion, or themselves had been apprentices at the Royal Exchange.[4] . . .

In some things the artists of India outdo all the ingenuity of Europe, viz. in the painting of chintzes or calicoes, which in Europe cannot be paralleled, either in the brightness and life of the colors, or in their continuance upon the cloth.[5] The gold stripes likewise in their sooseys, and the gold flowers in their atlases are imitated with us [i.e., by us],[6] but not to perfection. . . .

The English East India Company . . . are at the annual expense of one hundred thousand pounds. For they esteem it necessary, as well for the honor of the English nation, as facilitating of their traffic, to maintain their principal servants in India, not only in decency, but splendor, as is visible to any that has travelled either to Surat, or the Fort of St. George, to Gombroon in Persia, or Bengal. These are the chief places of note and trade, where their presidents and agents reside, for the support of whom, with their writers and factors, large privileges and salaries are allowed. . . .

Each day there is prepared a public table for the use of the President and the rest of the factory, who sit all down in a public place according to their seniority in the Company's service. The table is spread with the choicest meat[7] Surat affords, or the country thereabouts; and equal[ly] plenty of generous Shiraz wine, and arrack punch, is served round the table. Several hundreds a year are expended upon their daily provisions which are sumptuous enough for the entertainment of any person of eminence in the kingdom; and which require two or three cooks, and as many butchers to dress and prepare them. But Europe wines and English beer, because of their former acquaintance with our palates, are most coveted and most desirable liquors, and though sold at high rates, are yet purchased and drunk with pleasure. . . .

Both before and after meals, a peon appointed for that purpose attends with a large silver ewer and basin, for those that sit down to wash their hands; which at both times is a decency in all places, but here necessary, because of the heat and dust which are so very troublesome.

---

[3] A commode was a tall headdress fashionable with elite European women in the last third of the seventeenth century.

[4] The Royal Exchange was a London commercial and merchant center famous for millinery and, apparently, hairdressers.

[5] Ovington is referring here to the permanence of the dye.

[6] In short, imitation runs in both directions.

[7] This refers to food in general, not just to "meat" in the sense that we think of it.

All the dishes and plates brought to the table are of pure silver, massy and substantial; and such are also the tosses or cups out of which we drink. And that nothing may be wanting to please the curiosity of every palate at the times of eating, an English, Portuguese, and an Indian cook are all entertained to dress the meat in different ways for the gratification of every stomach. . . .

Upon Sundays and public days, the entertainments keep up a face of more solemnity, and are made more large and splendid, deer and antelopes, peacocks, hares, partridges, and all kind of Persian fruits, pistachios, plums, apricots, cherries, &c are all provided upon high festivals; and European as well as Persian wines are drunk with temperance and alacrity. . . .

The President upon solemn days generally invites the whole factory abroad to some pleasant garden adjacent to the city, where they may sit shaded from the beams of the sun, and refreshed by the neighborhood [i.e., proximity] of tanks and water-works. The President and his lady are brought hither in palanquins [i.e., litters or sedan chairs], supported each of them by six peons, which carry them by four at once on their shoulders. Before him at a little distance, are carried two large flags, or English ensigns, with curious Persian or Arabian horses of state, which are of great value, rich in their trappings, and gallantly equipped that are led before him. . . .

The evenings and the mornings being allayed with moderate breezes, and cool and temperate in respect of the heat when the sun is at the height, invite the factors daily almost to the groves or gardens near the water side, there to spend an hour or two with a bottle of wine, and cold collation which they carry with them. And neither the chaplain nor any of the Council stir without the walls of the city without the attendance of four or five peons upon the coach. This creates a respect from the natives as they pass along, strikes them with a regard to the English wherever they meet them, [and] makes them value our friendship, and place an honor in our intimacy and acquaintance. . . .

The factors when they eat at home, do it after the English manner, but abroad they imitate the customs of the East in lying round the banquet upon the Persian carpets which are spread upon the ground, twenty or thirty foot in length. . . .

And that both the Company and their servants may be constantly blessed with the favors of heaven upon them in their respective stations, therefore they have ordered a form of prayer to be used daily in their factories, for the obtaining a common blessing upon them all; which is as follows:

Oh Almighty and most merciful God, who art the sovereign protector of all that trust in thee, and the author of all spiritual and temporal blessings, we thy unworthy creatures do most humbly implore thy goodness for a plentiful effusion of thy Grace upon our employers, thy servants, the Right Honorable East India Company of England. Prosper them in all their public undertakings, and make them famous and successful in all their governments, colonies, and commerce both by sea and land; so that they may prove a public blessing by the increase of honor, wealth and power to our native country as well as to themselves. Continue their favors towards us, and inspire their generals, presidents, agents and councils in these remote parts of the world, and all others that are entrusted with any authority under them, with piety towards thee our God, and with wisdom, fidelity, and circumspection in their several stations; that we may all discharge our effective duties faithfully, and live virtuously, in due obedience to our superiors, and in love, peace and charity one towards another; that these Indian nations among whom we dwell, seeing our sober and righteous conversation, may be induced to have a just esteem for our most holy profession of the gospel of our lord and savior Jesus Christ, to whom be honor, praise and glory, now and forever. Amen.

2

Charter Granted by Charles II to the East India Company, Confirming and Extending Their Former Charters

April 3, 1661

Though originally given by Elizabeth I in 1600, the East India Company's charter underwent several revisions and amendments under subsequent regimes. The primary purpose of such a charter of incorporation was to confirm the East India Company as a legal entity and (in parts not reproduced here) to detail its governance procedures. But the letters patent (state documents issued by the monarch) also provide for particular constitutional rights and immunities similar to those offered both to other

John Shaw, *Charters Relating to the East India Company from 1600 to 1761, Reprinted from a Former Collection with Some Additions and a Preface* (Madras: Government Press, 1887), 32–33, 36–37, 39–40, 44–45.

overseas traders and to charters for plantations and colonies, including the right to export large amounts of specie, seize English subjects infringing on the monopoly, establish fortifications, set up courts, and exact reprisals on non-Christians.

Know ye, therefore, that We taking the Premises in Our Royal Consideration, and well weighing how highly it imports the Honor and Welfare of this Our Realm, and of Our good Subjects thereof, . . . have of Our especial Grace, certain Knowledge and mere Motion, and at the humble Petition of The said *Governor and Company*, given, granted, ratified and confirmed . . . unto Our said Trusty and well-beloved Subjects, The *Governor and Company of Merchants of London, Trading into the East-Indies*, that they from henceforth for ever be and shall be One Body Corporate and Politick, in Deed and in Name . . . And by the same name . . . capable in Law. . . .

And further We do, by these Presents, for Us, Our Heirs and Successors, will and grant unto The said *Governor and Company of Merchants of London, Trading into the East-Indies*, and their Successors, that they . . . shall and may, from henceforth for ever . . . freely traffick, and use the Trade of Merchandize by Seas, in and by such Ways and Passages, already found out and discovered, or which hereafter shall be found out and discovered, as they shall esteem and take to be fittest, into and from the said *East-Indies*, in the Countries and Parts of *Asia* and *Africa*, and into and from the Islands, Ports, Havens, Cities, Creeks, Towns and Places of *Asia*, *Africa*, and *America*, or any of them, beyond the *Cape of Bona Esperanza*, to the Straits of *Magellan*, where any Trade or Traffick of Merchandize may be used or had. . . .

And further . . . that they and their Successors, and their Factors, Servants and Assigns, in the Trade of Merchandize . . . shall for ever hereafter have, use, and enjoy, the whole entire and only Trade and Traffick, and the whole entire and only Liberty, Use and Privilege of trading and trafficking, and using the Seat and Trade of Merchandize, to and from the said *East-Indies*, and to and from all the Islands, Ports, Havens, Cities, Towns and Places aforesaid, in such Manner and Form as is above-mentioned. . . .

And further of Our especial Grace, certain Knowledge and mere Motion, We do, for Us, Our Heirs and Successors, grant to and with The said *Governor and Company of Merchants of London, Trading into the East-Indies*, and their Successors, that all Plantations, Forts, Fortifications, Factories or Colonies, where the said Company's Factories and

Trade are or shall be in the said *East-Indies*, shall be immediately and from henceforth under the Power and Command of The said *Governor and Company*, their Successors and Assigns; and that The said *Governor and Company of Merchants of London, Trading into the East-Indies*, shall have Liberty, full Power and Authority to appoint and establish Governors, and all other Officers to govern them: And that the Governor and his Council, of the several and respective Places where the said Company have, or shall have any Factories or Places of Trade, within the said *East-Indies*, may have Power to judge all Persons, belonging to The said *Governor and Company*, or that shall live under them, in all Causes, whether civil or criminal, according to the Laws of this Kingdom, and to execute Judgment accordingly. . . .

And moreover . . . We do give and grant unto The said *Governor and Company of Merchants of London, Trading into the East-Indies*, and their Successors, free Liberty and License for The said *Governor and Company*, in case they conceive it necessary to send either Ships of War, Men or Ammunition, into any [of] their Factories or other Places of their Trade, in the said *East-Indies*, for the Security and Defense of the same: And to choose Commanders and Officers over them, and to give them Power and Authority, by Commissions under their Common Seal or otherwise, to continue or make Peace or War with any Prince or People, that are not Christians, in any Places of their Trade, as shall be most for the Advantage and Benefit of The said *Governor and Company*, and of their Trade: And also to right and recompense themselves, upon the Goods, Estate or People of those Parts, by whom The said *Governor and Company*, shall sustain any Injury, Loss or Damage, or upon any other People whatsoever, that shall any ways interrupt, wrong or injure them, in their said Trade, within the said Places, Territories and Limits, granted unto The said *Governor and Company*, or their Successors, by this Charter: And that it shall and may be lawful, to and for The said *Governor and Company*, and their Successors, from Time to Time, and at all Times from henceforth, to erect and build such Castles, Fortifications, Forts, Garrisons, Colonies or Plantations, at *St. Helena*,[1] as also elsewhere, within the Limits and Bounds of Trade, granted unto The said *Governor and Company*, as aforesaid, as they in their Discretions shall think fit and requisite. . . .

And further Our Will and Pleasure is, and by these Presents, for Us, Our Heirs and Successors, We do grant unto The said *Governor and*

---

[1] The South Atlantic island of St. Helena was first granted to the East India Company in 1658 by Richard Cromwell.

Company of Merchants of London, Trading into the East-Indies, and to their Successors, full Power and Lawful Authority, to seize upon the Persons of all such *English*, or any other Our Subjects, in the said *East-Indies*, which shall sail in any *Indian* or *English* Vessel, or inhabit in those Parts, without the Leave and License of The said *Governor and Company*, in that Behalf first had and obtained, or that shall contemn or disobey their Orders, and send them to *England*; and that all and every Person or Persons, being Our Subjects, any ways employed by The said *Governor and Company*, in the said *East-Indies*, or any other Place, within the Parts, Places and Limits, before by these Presents granted unto The said *Governor and Company*, shall be liable unto and suffer such Punishment, for any Offences, by them committed in the said *East-Indies*, and Parts before granted as the President and Council for The said *Governor and Company* there shall think fit, and the Merit of the Offence shall require.

3

Letters Patent from Charles II for the Port and Island of Bombay

March 27, 1669

In 1661, upon the marriage of the English king Charles II to the Portuguese princess Catherine of Braganza, and as part of a larger peace treaty and alliance against the Dutch, Portugal granted to the English monarch "direct, full and absolute dominion and sovereignty" over both the North African port of Tangier and the western Indian "island" of Bombay. While it tried, with disastrous results, to rule at Tangier, the English government very quickly transferred Bombay to the East India Company. These patents are similar in form to many documents issued for colonies in the Americas, as well as to those issued by Charles II in 1674 for the Company's proprietorship over the South Atlantic island of

Charters Granted to the East-India Company, from 1601; Also the Treaties and Grants, Made with, or Obtained from, the Princes and Powers in India, from the Year 1756 to 1772 (London, 1773), 80–85, 87–89, 91.

St. Helena. The charter spelled out the East India Company's rights and responsibilities on the island, which included the establishment of warlike provisions, the recruitment of soldiers, the establishment of laws, and the execution of punishments (including capital punishment), all issues that blurred the line between the commercial functions of the Company and its role as a government over the colony.

Charles the Second, by the Grace of God, King of *England, Scotland, France*, and *Ireland*, Defender of the Faith, etc. . . .

[We] do give, grant, transfer and confirm, unto The said *Governor and Company of Merchants of London Trading into the East Indies*, their Successors and Assigns, all that the [*sic*] said Port and Island *Bombay*, in the *East-Indies*, with all the Rights, Profits, Territories and Appurtenances thereof whatsoever: And all and singular Royalties, Revenues, Rents, Customs, Castles, Forts, Buildings and Fortifications, Privileges, Franchises, Preheminences and Hereditaments whatsoever, within the said Premises, or to them or any of them belonging, or in any wise appertaining, in as large and ample Manner, to all Intents, Constructions and Purposes, as We Ourselves now have and enjoy, or may or ought to have and enjoy the same, by Virtue and Force of the said Grant of Our said Brother, the King of *Portugal*, and not further or otherwise; and them The said *Governor and Company of Merchants of London, Trading into the East-Indies*, their Successors and Assigns, We do, by these Presents, for Us, Our Heirs and Successors, make, create, and constitute, the true and absolute Lords and Proprietors of the Port and Island, and Premises aforesaid, and of every Part and Parcel thereof, . . . as of the Manor of *East-Greenwich*, in the County of *Kent*,[1] in free and common Soccage,[2] and not in Capite,[3] nor by Knight's Service, yielding and paying therefore to Us, Our Heirs and Successors, at the *Custom-House, London*, the Rent or Sum of Ten Pounds of lawful Money of *England*, in Gold, on the Thirtieth Day of September, yearly, for ever. . . .

And we do also confirm and grant unto The said *Governor and Company*, and their Successors . . . to have Power and Authority of Government or Command, in and over the said Port and Island: . . . to use and

---

[1] A legal formula, derived from feudal land-tenure grants, common in England, as well as in American charters.

[2] in socage: Land held in return for payment of rent, rather than forms of service such as a military obligation.

[3] in capite: Lands held directly by the King; land tenures in capite were abolished by Act of Parliament in 1660.

exercise all such Powers and Authorities, in cases of Rebellion, Mutiny or Sedition, of refusing to serve in Wars, flying to the Enemy, forsaking Colors or Ensigns, or other Offences, against Law, Custom and Discipline Military, in as large and ample Manner, to all Intent and Purposes whatsoever, as any Captain General of Our Army, by Virtue of his Office have used and accustomed, and may or might lawfully do. . . .

4

Letters Patent from James II Extending Jurisdiction of Prize Courts in the East Indies
April 12, 1686

One of the biggest challenges facing the East India Company in the late seventeenth century was the threat from interlopers—English subjects living and trading in Asia without the Company's permission and often hostile to its purposes. Though the Company's charters had always given it the authority to establish laws and judicature courts, it had lobbied for some time to have authority from the king to prosecute interlopers in India and to seize and condemn booty from their ships, rather than having to wait to do so in Europe. In 1683, the Company received such a license from Charles II, in the form of letters patent authorizing the East India Company to establish its own law courts in South Asia. In 1686, James II, who succeeded Charles II in 1685, confirmed and expanded the power of those courts, which came to deal not only with interloper and piracy "prizes" but also with confiscations made within the context of war.

And further We do, for Us, Our Heirs and Successors, by these Presents, erect and establish a Court of Judicature, to be held at such Place or Places, Fort or Forts, Plantations or Factories, upon the Coasts before recited, within the Limits of any of the before recited Charters, as the said Company shall, from Time to Time, direct and appoint; which

Charters Granted to the East-India Company, from 1601; Also the Treaties and Grants, Made with, or Obtained from, the Princes and Powers in India, from the Year 1756 to 1772 (London, 1773), 136–39.

Court . . . shall have Commission and Power to hear and determine all Causes of Forfeitures and Seizures of any Ship or Ships, Goods and Merchandize, trading and coming upon any the said Coasts or Limits, contrary to the Intent of these Presents, or of the First recited Letters Patents; and also all Causes, mercantile or maritime, Bargains, buyings, sellings, bartering of Wares whatsoever, and all Policies and Acts of Assurance; all Bonds, Bills, and Promises for Payment of Money, or mercantile or trading Contracts, all Charter-Parties, or trading Contracts for affreighting of Vessels, and Wages of Mariners, and all other mercantile or maritime Cases, or Cases of Reprisals of Ships or Goods, for any Hurt or Damage done to the said Company, by any Person or Persons whatsoever, and all other maritime Cases whatsoever, concerning any Person or Persons residing, coming or being in the Places aforesaid, and all Cases of Trespasses, Injuries and Wrongs, done or committed upon the High Sea, or in any of the Regions, Territories or Places aforesaid, within the Limits of the First recited Letters Patents of the said late King *Charles* the Second, concerning any Person or Persons residing, being or coming in the Parts of *Asia*, or *Africa*, within the Bounds and Limits aforesaid. . . .

And further, whereas We are also given to understand, that many of the native Princes and Governors of *India*, and other Nations, taking Opportunity from the Divisions, Distractions or Rebellions, amongst the *English*, occasioned by the late licentious trading of Interlopers, have of late violated many of the Company's Privileges, surprised their Servants, Ships and Goods, besieged their Factories, invaded their Liberties, and [in] many other Ways, without just Cause, greatly endamaged and abused their Chiefs and Factors, to the Dishonor of the *English* Nation in those Parts of the World; for which Injuries and Damages, the said Company intend[s] to demand and procure Satisfaction in a peaceable Way, if in that Manner it be attainable; and if not, then the said Company intend[s] to endeavor the Recovery of their Loss and Damages, and to procure their Satisfaction, by Force of Arms, wherein they will have Occasion to use their Ships in a Warlike Manner; and have thereupon humbly besought Us, that in Time of War, or actual Hostility, with any Nation in the *East-Indies*, they may use and exercise the Law, commonly called the Law Martial, as well in their Ships as in any their Plantations, Forts and Places, within the Limits of their respective Charters aforesaid, for Defense of their said Ships, against any foreign Enemy or domestic Insurrection, Rebellion or Disorder. We do therefore, for Us, Our Heirs and Successors, further give and grant full Power, License and Authority, to the said Governor, Deputy, and Court of the said Company, for the Time being, or the major Part of them, duly assembled, to name and appoint Admirals, Vice-Admirals, Rear-Admirals, Captains and other Sea Officers, from Time to Time, in all or any Ship or Ships serving the said Company, in the said *East-Indies*, within the Limits of any of the above recited Charters. . . . [And] We do, for Us, Our Heirs and Successors, give them hereby full Power, License, Commission and Authority, to raise, arm, train and muster such Number of Seamen, or other Military Soldiers, as to them shall seem necessary, on board their respective Ships, or as they shall be ordered and directed by The said *Governor and Company*, or their Successors, or the Captain General of the *English*, in *India*, appointed or to be appointed by The said *Governor and Company*, and to exercise and use, within their Ships on the other Side of the *Cape of Good Hope*, in the Time of open Hostility with some other Nation, the Law, called the Law Martial, for Defense of their Ships, against the Enemy.

2

Mughal Expansion under the Emperor Aurangzeb

5

ISHWAR DAS NAGAR

Modes of Siege Warfare—and Restoring Order Afterward

1688

This excerpt describes an attack by the Mughals on an especially strong fort, Fort Adoni, located about two hundred miles east of Goa on the border between the modern Indian states of Andhra Pradesh and Karnataka. The story displays some striking parallels with Sidi Yakut's Siege of Bombay. One spark (or pretext) for war, as in the case of Bombay, was the fort's governor having stopped grain shipments meant for the imperial army. The author of this account, Ishwar das Nagar, was a Brahmin from Gujarat who worked in various capacities for the Mughal legal and courtly bureaucracy and who was ultimately given a mansab by Aurangzeb. Sidi Masud Khan, the defeated noble, was, like Sidi Yakut, of African descent. He had been wazir (chief minister) in the Bijapur Sultanate, a Muslim regime that fell to Aurangzeb's forces in the 1680s. Sidi Masud Khan had apparently sought to establish himself independently at Fort Adoni, but he was thwarted by Aurangzeb.

Ishwar das Nagar, *Futuhat-i-Alamgiri*, translated from the Persian by M. F. Lokhandwala and Sir Jadunath Sarkar. Edited by Raghubir Sinh and Quazi Karamtullah (Vadodara, India: Oriental Institute, 1995), 128–31.

Capture of the Adoni Fort

ARRIVAL OF THE IMPERIAL CAMP AT BIJAPUR AND THE COMING OF THE HAPPY NEWS OF THE CAPTURE OF FORT ADONI

The Emperor [Aurangzeb] decided to visit Bijapur. So, beginning his march at an auspicious hour by crossing stages, in twenty-five days he reached Bijapur. . . .

At this time, came the news of the capture of Fort Adoni, belonging to Bijapur, through the exertions of the Imperialists [i.e., the Mughals]. The following is a short account of it:

The fort of Adoni had no second in strength; it was in the hands of Sidi Masud. As the Emperor at this time repeatedly learnt that the wretch had stepped out of the position of obedience, collected a body of foolish adventurers, raised the banner of disorder, and stationing a party on the bank of the river, had stopped the path of the coming grain [to the imperial camp], so that, at this occurrence Ghaziuddin Khan Bahadur with his detachment arrived 20 kos[1] from Adoni with a view to punish the wretch and encamped. The enemy's troops daily stepped into the field with materials of war and fought with the Imperialists. Moreover owing to the scarcity of grain, the Imperial army was greatly overcome by hardship and famine.

The Emperor ordered that Rustam Khan and Fatih Jang Khan, with a large detachment, should quickly go and join Firuz Jang Khan and punish the rebel. When the two Khans arrived on the scene, the enemy engaged in fighting, but being worsted fled away. Then Firuz Jang Khan sent Rustam Khan to capture Fort Sanchuli, and Fatih Jang Khan to besiege Fort Harkumar, close to Adoni, and [to stop] the coming of grain and other materials, that used to reach the fort of Adoni from that place. The two Khans after reconnecting both the forts captured them after a fight, and sent their keys with dispatches to His Majesty. Then the qiladars[2] were appointed to them from the Court. At this the Sidi's composure was disturbed, his heart was shaken, and his firmness gone. Firuz Jang Khan, after the two Khans rejoined him, arrived at Adoni, encamped one or two kos from the fort, and began to prepare requisites of a siege, such as mines and covered lanes. At this the Sidi became very anxious; he saw no way of flight, and being seized with confusion by reason of the greatness of his alarm, desperately set his heart on death and

---

[1] A kos was a unit of measurement corresponding to between 1⅛ and 2¼ miles, depending on the region.

[2] Qil'adar, from Arabic ḳal'a, "a fort"; the commandant of a fort, castle, or garrison.

his body on battle, began violence and tumult, and deputed a large force to fight the Imperialists. They began battle. At this Firuz Jang Khan adopted this contrivance that he with expert soldiers lay in ambush amidst the dense trees, sent Muhammad Salih, his chief officer [or adviser], with another force towards the back of the fort and appointed a body of soldiers to confront the enemy. When this body, ascending the top of a hill, revealed themselves to view, the enemy, finding them to be a small body, recklessly galloped up to them. The Imperialists stood firmly and after striking some blows on the enemy's arrival, turned their reins towards their camp. The enemy boldly gave chase; but when they reached this plain, Khan Firuz Jang from this side and Muhammad Salih from that side arrived at a gallop, grappled with the enemy and fought furiously. In the end Muhammad Salih fell fighting with 150 of his men; many were wounded. Many of the enemy were slain; and the rest fled. The Emperor, on hearing of the victory, presented Firuz Jang Khan with a jeweled aigrette and purkhanah and one elephant and two horses, and Rustam Khan and Fatih Jang Khan each with a special robe of honor and one horse. Firuz Jang Khan urged him to leave no trace of trees for a distance of three or four kos from the fort, so that the enemy might despair of such shelter, . . . and also to ride against the enemy for 15 kos [from the fort to] the neighborhood of the river, who were comrades of this wretch [Sidi Masud], and capture their families and children. As the enemy interfered with the arrival of grain, he set up four outposts at distances of 15 kos, from Adoni to Bijapur, which were 60 kos apart, in order to enable travelers to pass freely. When the mine and covered lane reached the foot of the fort, the wives and children of the musketeers guarding the fort, who dwelt there, were made prisoners. So one of the chiefs of the musketeers sought protection and on the strength of Khan Firuz Jang's safe conduct visited him and told him, "If our wives and children are kept in one place and not one of them scattered, and none does dishonor [to] them, we shall open the gate of the fort and deliver it to the Imperialists. But after the capture of the fort you will deliver our families up to us." Firuz Jang Khan agreed to the request and conciliated him. But when Sidi Masud learnt of it from the report of his spies (harkaras), he became paralyzed and senseless with fear, and knowing that he had no means of deliverance except submission to the Emperor, helplessly sent one of his chief officers with all humility and submission to ask for an Imperial letter promising him safety and stamped with the emperor's palm. He also submitted that he was delivering the fort to Khan Firuz Jang and the Khan should write to the Emperor that some place in the wide kingdom of the Deccan might be assigned for his subsistence as he had many dependents, and that he would live peacefully in that corner as a devoted servant of the Court.

At this time Sidi Khan Muhammad, the son of Sidi Masud, came, interviewed Firuz Jang Khan, delivered to him the key of the fort[3] and recited the following couplet: "To thee I deliver my all; Thou knowest the calculation of more or less."

The Khan soothed his frightened heart by all means, called him his son, laid his hand lovingly on his head, bowed in humility to the Omnipotent, rendered the thanks to Him many times, and sent back to Sidi Masud the message that he was sending to Court a dispatch with a wajib-ul-arz[4] containing the Sidi's prayer, but that the Sidi should remain in the fort till the arrival of a reply and the acceptance of his terms. Firuz Jang sent to the Emperor a dispatch congratulating him on the capture of the fort together with its gold key, and a wajib-ul-arz stating the demands of the Sidi, as well as 1,000 mohars[5] as nazar.[6] The Emperor sent a gracious farman promising safety and adorned with the stamp of his palm and a sanad[7] conferring the fort of Mudgal[8] in al-tamgha[9] for the residence of the Sidi's family by the hand of Abdus Samad, mace-bearer. Sidi Masud was created a commander of 7,000 (5,000 troopers), his son Sidi Khan Muhammad a commander of 5,000 (3,000 troopers) and his officers and connections received mansabs corresponding to their condition and rank. Firuz Jang sent the farman and the sanad to the Sidi, who advanced to welcome the farman and the hereditary sanad, made his obeisance [to them], took the two papers, gave to the mace-bearer a remuneration of a robe, one horse, and 2,000 hun,[10] and issuing from the fort went to see Firuz Jang Khan, who on hearing of the Sidi's coming, laid out a grand majlis,[11] stationed the nobles present with him in their respective positions, [and] drew up his troops in ranks at the door of his tent-screen with great pomp. When Sidi Masud arrived near the tent-screen, Firuz Jang Khan, with great politeness and respect, rose up

[3] The fort of Adoni was captured on August 5, 1688.

[4] wajib-ul-arz: In this context, a petition.

[5] mohar or mohur: Gold coin in wide use under the Mughals. In 1690, it was said to be worth around 14 silver rupees.

[6] nazar: A ceremonial present, especially from an inferior to a superior; from the Arabic and Persian.

[7] sanad: A patent or deed of grant by the government of an office, a privilege, or a right, or, in this case, an estate.

[8] The Mudgal Fort was, in fact, located quite close to Adoni.

[9] al-tamgha: A type of Mughal land tenure that was generally free from revenue assessment and indicated hereditary possession; from Turkic.

[10] hun: A gold coin (also called a pagoda).

[11] majlis: Gathering (literally, sitting place); from the Arabic.

and advanced to the middle of the carpet to welcome him, embraced him and with great honor seated him on the cushion, spent one prahar[12] in his company, fed him hospitably with all kinds of food, drink and fruits, and gave him leave to go at the close of the day. Then he entered the fort with Rustam Khan, Fatih Jang Khan and other nobles and gave Sidi Masud permission to go to Fort Mudgal. The Sidi went out for that place, leaving his son Sidi (Muhammad) Jan [and] other relatives and near ones at the service of Firuz Jang Khan. The Emperor on hearing of it presented to Firuz Jang Khan a splendid robe of honor, a jeweled sarpech,[13] one elephant and two horses, while the other commanders were rewarded with increment of rank and in other ways. On the occurrence of this grand victory, Prince Muhammad Azam Shah offered one thousand *mohars* and the nobles other sums according to their means and rank, by way of niyaz and nazar.[14] The music of victory was played.

[12] prahar: A unit of time meaning a quarter of a day or night.
[13] sarpech: An ornament worn in front of a turban.
[14] Niyaz and nazar in combination mean vows and oblations (or offerings); from the Persian and Arabic.

6

Capture of Orchha

1635

This image comes from the Padshahnama, *or chronicle of the reign of the Mughal emperor Shah Jahan (r. 1628–1658), which was written by Abdul Hamid Lahori. The image was painted sometime between 1635 and 1647. It depicts the 1635 siege and capture of the fort of Orchha in the modern-day Indian state of Madhya Pradesh in the aftermath of a rebellion. The attack, led by a teenaged Aurangzeb, offers a vivid picture not only of the future emperor's personal military experience but also of the typical experience of a fort besieged by overwhelming Mughal military force.*

7

The Emperor Aurangzeb at a Chishti Shrine
1670s

This image probably dates from the 1670s and depicts Emperor Aurangzeb, who was known for his piety, visiting the shrine of the Chishti Sufi saint, Muinuddin Chishti, in Ajmer (a city in the present-day Indian state of Rajasthan). To the right of the picture, in profile, are some of Aurangzeb's family members. To the left is a group of lesser courtiers, including a Sidi and at least one person of Central Asian origin.

Mead Art Museum/Bridgeman Art Library

3

Sidi Yakut Khan and Rising Tension in Bombay

8

KHAFI KHAN

On Sidi Yakut

1670s–1680s

East Africans, referred to in regional parlance as "Sidis," had been arriving in India for centuries, some as traders and many as slaves. Over time, a number of them had acquired high political and military offices. Sidi Yakut of Janjira (d. 1707), who orchestrated and led the Siege of Bombay, had originally been associated with the Bijapur Sultanate but by the time of the siege had moved into the orbit of the Mughal Empire. Muhammad Hashim, better known as Khafi Khan, was born to a good family, his father having worked for the emperor Aurangzeb in both military and civil capacities, as would Khafi Khan himself. This excerpt from his famous "unauthorized" history of the Mughal dynasty focuses on Sidi Yakut's military skills but also stresses the Sidi's complicated character, his long-standing quarrel with the Marathas, and his possession of the famously impregnable fortress of Janjira, south of Bombay. Khafi Khan's account also demonstrates the fluid and hybrid nature of political and military power in the Mughal Empire, a place where a talented individual of African descent could amass power, prestige, and territory.

Khafi Khan, *Muntakhab-al-Lubab*, excerpted in John Dowson, ed. and trans., *The History of India as Told by Its Own Historians* (London: Trübner and Co., 1877), 7:289–92.

Fateh Khan, an Afghan,[1] was appointed governor of the country on the part of Bijapur, and he posted himself in the fort of Danda-Rajpuri,[2] which is situated half in the sea and half on land. Subsequently he built the fort of Janjira[3] upon an island in the sea, about a cannon-shot distant from Danda-Rajpuri, in a very secure position, so that, if the governor of the country was hard pressed by an enemy, he might have a secure retreat in that place. After Sivaji had fixed his abode at Rahiri, which is twenty kos from Danda-Rajpuri, he appointed a commandant of that fortress. In a short time, he reduced [i.e., conquered] and occupied seven other forts, small and great, in that neighborhood, and then resolved upon the conquest of Danda-Rajpuri. Fateh Khan had observed the triumphant progress of Sivaji, and how fortress after fortress had fallen into his hands. So Fateh Khan lost courage; he abandoned Danda-Rajpuri, and retired to the island fortress in the sea. Sivaji then resolved to effect the conquest of the island also, and he so conducted matters that Fateh Khan was soon reduced to extremities, and he offered to surrender the place to Sivaji, upon a pledge of security to himself and the garrison.

Fateh Khan had in his service three Abyssinian slaves, Sidi Sambal, Sidi Yakut, and Sidi Khairiyat, each of whom had ten Abyssinian slaves, which he had trained and drilled. The management of the island and of many domestic concerns was in the hands of these Abyssinians.[4] These three men got information of the enemy's power, and of Fateh Khan's intention of surrendering the island to Sivaji. They took counsel together, and resolved that no good could come from allowing the island to pass into the hands of any infidel. So they determined to take Fateh Khan prisoner, and to make Sidi Sambal governor of the fortress. In the fourteenth year of the reign these Abyssinians seized Fateh Khan unawares, placed chains upon his legs, and wrote a statement of the facts to Adil Shah Bijapuri. They also wrote to Khan-Jahan, the Subadar of the Deccan,[5] begging the aid of the Imperial forces, and requesting him to send his forces by sea from Surat. Khan-Jahan graciously bestowed mansabs and presents on each of the three Abyssinians. . . .

---

[1] Some sources say that Fateh Khan was actually a Sidi, not an Afghan.

[2] The twin towns of Danda and Rajpuri are about 50 miles down the coast from Bombay. For a large portion of the period of Fateh Khan's command, the fort was besieged by Maratha forces.

[3] Here spelled Jazira (meaning "island" in Arabic).

[4] It has been argued that the three Sidis were not slaves but members of the local Janjira nobility.

[5] Here Subadar means a provincial governor within the Mughal Empire; from Persian: ṣūbadār, or province-holder.

Sivaji collected forty or fifty vessels of war to defend the forts of Kalaba and Gandiri, which were the strongest of his newly-built forts on the sea-shore. He then turned his thoughts to the reduction of the fort of Janjira, and the capture of the Abyssinians. There were frequent naval fights between the opposing forces, in which the Abyssinians were often victorious. Sidi Sambal was advanced to a mansab of 900, and then he died. Before he expired he made Sidi Yakut his successor, and enjoined all the other Abyssinians to pay him a loyal and cheerful obedience. Sidi Yakut was distinguished among his people for benignity and dignity. He now strove more than ever to collect ships of war, to strengthen the fortress, and to ward off naval attacks. He was armed and ready night and day. He frequently captured ships of the enemy, and cut off the heads of many Marathas, and sent them to Surat. He used to write reports to Khan-Jahan, and he frequently received marks of approbation from him. He was constantly revolving in his mind plans for wresting the fort of Danda-Rajpuri[6] from the hands of Sivaji. He got together some rockets which he fastened to trees, and discharged them at night against the fort.

Sivaji also was prosecuting his plans for the reduction of Janjira. But he now retired to a dwelling about three kos [away] to celebrate the holi,[7] leaving in command at Rajpuri some officers experienced in siege work, to prosecute incessantly the operations against Janjira during his absence, and he held out to them the reward of a man of gold and other presents. One night, while the garrison of Danda-Rajpuri were celebrating the holi, and were intoxicated or inattentive, Sidi Yakut sent on shore four or five hundred men under Sidi Khairiyat with ropes, ladders and other apparatus. He himself drew thirty or forty boats laden with siege materiel under the walls of Rajpuri, and gave the signal agreed upon to announce his arrival. They found the garrison off their guard, and Sidi Khairiyat assaulted the place with loud cries from the land side. When the enemy took the alarm, and rushed to repel the attack on that side, Sidi Yakut planted his scaling-ladders, which he had brought in his boats, and by means of these and of ropes, his brave followers scaled the walls, and quickly made their way up. Some of the assailants were cast into the sea, and were drowned, others fell under the swords of the defenders, but the storming party forced its way into the fort, and raised the cry, "Strike! Kill!" Just at this time the powder magazine caught fire,

[6]This fort was very close to Janjira but on the mainland.
[7]A Hindu religious festival associated with spring and with feasting, dancing, and playing with colors.

and blew up a number of men, including ten or twelve who were with Sidi Yakut. The smoke and the noise made it difficult to distinguish friend from foe, but Sidi Yakut raised his war-cry, and encouraged his men to slaughter the defenders who had escaped the fire. Sidi Khairiyat also scaled the walls on his side, and the place was taken.

I, the author, was in that country some time, and I repeatedly heard from many men; and from the mouth of [Sidi] Yakut Khan himself, that when the magazine blew up, although Sivaji was twenty kos off, it awoke him from sleep, and he said that some misfortune had fallen on Danda-Rajpuri, and he sent men to ascertain what had happened.

At this time Sivaji's forces had gone to attack the neighborhood of Surat. Within the space of four or five kos from Rajpuri there were six or seven Nizam-ul-Mulki forts which had fallen into the hands of Sivaji, but he was unable at this time to render them any assistance. So Sidi Yakut seized the opportunity to attack them. Six forts surrendered after two or three days' resistance, but the commandant of one fort held out for a week in the hope of relief from Sivaji. The Abyssinians pushed forward their approaches, and kept up such a fire that he was obliged to surrender. Sidi Yakut granted quarter to the garrison, and seven hundred persons came out. But notwithstanding his word, he made the children and pretty women slaves, and forcibly converted them to Islam. The old and ugly women he set free, but the men he put to death. This struck such terror into the hearts of Sivaji and his followers that he [Sivaji] was obliged to confine himself to securing Rahiri. Sidi Yakut sent an account of his victory to Prince Muhammad Mu'azzam, subadar of the Deccan, and to Khan-Jahan. His mansab was raised, a robe of honor was sent to him; and he received the title of Khan. Similar honors were also given to Sidi Khairiyat.

9

Murder in the Bazaar: Clashes between Englishmen and the Sidi's Soldiers

1683

The English East India Company's troubles with Sidi Yakut long preceded the invasion of the island in 1689. In this routine letter to their superiors in London, the members of the Company's governing council in Surat report on a conflict at Bombay's bazaar (central market) between a soldier in the Sidi's employ and two Englishmen, in which one of the Englishmen died. Despite the Company's desire to arrest and publicly execute the man for murder, he safely returned to the Sidi's ship. This in turn led a Company captain and two others to an absurd (and drunken) attempt to retrieve him. The frictions between the Sidi's sailors and the residents at Bombay were nothing new, the Sidi having wintered his fleet at Bombay frequently since the 1670s, putting great strain on the island's provisions and its relationship with the neighboring Marathas.

The Sidi this past rains [i.e., monsoon season, or June to early September] hath been very abusive, and troublesome at Bombay. Some of his Pathans[1] quarreled [with] two English men in the bazaar, [and] wounded both of them. One whereof [was] deceased in very few days purely out of his wounds; the other recovered. It made a very great disturbance. The deputy governor and council demanded the murderer but could not obtain his being delivered to them. We likewise made our addresses to this governor [the mutasaddi[2] of Surat], who promised us satisfaction, and looked on our demands to be very just and reasonable, that we had a plain prospect of attaining our desires in having the Pathan executed publicly at Bombay, which was what we aimed at to deter the Sidi's men from such like actions from the future, remove all

[1] Pathans, or Pashtuns: Afghan military labor in the employ of the Sidi.
[2] The mutasaddi, as head of the port, was the chief civilian Mughal official in Surat, and the English often referred to him as the "governor" or "nabob" (nawab).

Surat Council to London, November 30, 1683. British Library, India Office Records E/3/43 fols. 205–6.

grudging and heart burnings of our own people, and by that to preserve a fair understanding with the Sidi, but we were soon off from prosecuting this by an action so strange as hardly to be believed. And indeed we do the more admire at it since Captain Consett being with us, who hath behaved himself extraordinary well here, and appears a man of ingenuity and understanding not at all given to drink, nor in the least seemingly passionate. . . .

The captain took his boat and with his chief mate went on board the Sidi's ship. Soon after him followed Nicholls, that naughty turbulent man, in the ship's yawl;[3] pretending to fetch the captain back, but by what we can gather was a great promoter of the mischief. An account of it we have several ways, from the deputy governor and council, the captain himself, and Mr. Henry Smith, etc. But the best excuse can be made for the captain, etc., is bad enough. On board the Sidi's ship they quarreled. Nicholls drew [his sword] and slightly wounded a man, and it cannot be thought had the Sidi a mind to mischief them having then no less than 3 in 400 men aboard, could easily have done what he pleased with three: two naked [i.e., unarmed] men and the other [armed with] a foolish little sword. The captain was slightly wounded in the knee, and as it's said hove [i.e., leaped or was thrown] overboard. The chief mate leaped over the quarter [deck rail]. Both got to their boat and Nicholls after all permitted to go fairly down the side. Immediately after [they] came on board their ship, [they] fired at the Sidi 11 great guns shotted [i.e., already loaded with shot]. But blessed be the divine goodness who wonderfully preserved you[r] affairs, and all our lives; for but 4 guns took place,[4] notwithstanding they were so near one another and they killed not one man and but slightly wounded 3 or 4 by the splinters flying. The cause of the captain going on board is represented to us by the deputy governor and council from a discourse that Mr. Henry Smith raised on board concerning a proclamation by the captain because of an affront offered his longboat. And Mr. Smith gives it in that he demanded of the Sidi the Pathan that murdered our Englishman, and forbid his beating his drums. However it is, the captain hath fallen into a great error, and put us to consider whither we should trust any of your concerns in his ship, but it was concluded to lade [i.e., load] her, the captain appearing very sensible of his fault and indeed very much troubled. So much we have seen in him, that we truly believe he will be more careful for the future.

---

[3]A two-masted yacht often used for fishing or as a ship's tender.
[4]This could mean that only four guns went off or perhaps that only four balls hit the Sidi's ship.

4

Company Plans for War

10

EAST INDIA COMPANY

A Fleet of Warlike Ships: Secret Instructions for War
March and April 1686

Amid the growing threat of interloping and the anticipation of war with Siam and the Mughal Empire in the early 1680s, the East India Company in London created a "secret committee," which was a powerful subcommittee of the "court of committees" (i.e., board of directors) dominated in this period by the London merchant and political economist Josiah Child. As its name suggests, the secret committee kept its proceedings and instructions secret from most of the rest of the East India Company stockholders, directors, and even some members of councils in India; sometimes even ships' captains (as in the document included here) were given specific instructions not to open their orders until well out to sea. The committee conceived of the idea of pressuring the Mughal emperor into making concessions by capturing Indian shipping, which in the long run would be one of the causes of the invasion. To that end, in 1686 they sent a large fleet of twenty-one ships out to India. Among the twenty-one were the five largest ships in the East India fleet. Altogether the ships carried 1,500 men and more than 600 cannon.

British Library, India Office Records E/3/91, fols. 48–49, 51.

Secret Committee Instructions to General and Council of Surat and Deputy Governor and Council of Bombay

... The Governor and Committees[1] having left it to us or any three of us, to give you such secret instructions, with our Sovereign Lord the King's approbation, as we think may tend most to his Majesty and his Kingdom's and the Company's honor and interest, in this time of trouble, and probable war in Bengal, we have thought it necessary to enclose with this all our Secret Instructions to Bengal and Fort St. George [Madras], and to the flag officers and other captains of our ships already gone upon that voyage to the intent you should know the necessity and true grounds of that great undertaking; And what orders we have given for the commencement & carrying on of that design.

And in regard [i.e., Since] we know Bengal is under the same great king's dominions as Surat is, and that our old friends the Dutch will be ready to interpose in this, or any other quarrel of ours (tho we never did in any of theirs) to do you what prejudice they can as well at Bombay as Surat, we have at our excessive charge sent out a considerable fleet of warlike ships for your assistance and defense. . . .

And in regard we do not know but our general[2] and council or some of our principal servants may be detained [i.e., imprisoned] by the Mughal's governor [i.e., the mutasaddi] at Surat,[3] by reason of our differences in Bengal, as also because on such occasions as those, it is good to ride the fore-horse if we can, we have ordered all our captains to [capture and] bring to Bombay, any of the Mughal's or his subjects' ships or junks that they can meet with in their passage, but not to take the value of a penny from any of them as they will answer the contrary at the peril of his Majesty's displeasure, until they are condemned[4] at Bombay, if it prove a war. But that they shall be released without losing the value of a penny, if our differences with the Mughal may be compounded in an amicable way.

We would have you, if it prove a war, reserve one sixth part of the proceeds of all prize ships and goods at sea, for the reward of commanders, officers, seamen, and soldiers, and for relief of wounded and maimed and the widows and orphans of such as shall be killed in this

[1]The court of committees, which was the executive council of the East India Company.

[2]John Child, governor of Bombay, who was also appointed "General" of the Company's forces in India.

[3]The Mughals did indeed imprison Company servants in Surat when the war broke out.

[4]Judged in prize court to be lawful seizures.

service, according to the order and discretion of any council of war for that purpose. . . .

We are so well satisfied of the fidelity and great abilities of our general by his 30 years' experience of and residence in India, that we shall give you no particular directions, but leave all to his and your prudence, to do whatever you think is most for the honour of our King and Country and for the Company's interest, remembering that we are merchants and must live by trade and not by a long war.

We have often wrote you according to the order of his late Majesty and council, after many years' conference concerning that, to pay no more custom at Tannah and Karinja, both, which places do of right belong to his Majesty [i.e., the English king]. But that if the Portugals do attempt to exact it of you by force, you should resist force with force, and if that business bring you into a war with them, it can never happen at a better time than this, now you are armed for other purposes, and therefore if you are put to it, and the Portugals be the aggressors, we would have you do your best to recover from them those adjacent islands to Bombay which belong to Bombay and were formerly dependencies upon Bombay (especially Salsette) and ought to have been delivered to his Majesty when Bombay was surrendered, for want whereof that island instead of being a benefit, hath been a dead charge to this Company first and last of at least 300,000 pound sterling, and can't possibly subsist for want of provisions, if you should be at any time blocked up by sea, without supply from the adjoining Salsette.

It will be necessary for you to make and always to keep a strict confederacy with Sambhaji Rajah,[5] who is a warlike prince and though he be not the most careful of his honour, or of keeping his leagues [i.e., treaties and alliances], all those Indian princes will keep their confederacys so long as they agree with their interests, and it's possible for you to make such terms with him, as shall be now and for many years his interest to sweeten him wherein, you may among other things agree to furnish him constantly with so much powder, great guns and shot and small arms on reasonable terms, as he shall desire annually, for which purpose we have now sent you a double proportion of powder and if you should want more, you may write for what you will to Fort St George [Madras], where we have 2600 barrels in store. . . . You may likewise send to President Gifford for 100 [Topass] soldiers if you want them, which may do you good service under English officers and be some

---

[5]Sambhaji Bhonsle (r. 1680–1689), the Maratha emperor, son of Sivaji.

balance to your Canareens and Rajputs[6] it being never good to have too many of one caste in arms under us.

East India Company Secret Committee Instructions to Captain Jonathan Andrews, Commander of the Charles II

April 24, 1686

. . . We do hereby order you to sail with what expedition you can for the Company's Island of Bombay, where you are to follow the orders of our general and council or of our general himself for the time being, who we have appointed to be our Captain General Admiral and Commander in Chief, of all the Company's forces by sea and land and as your next superior officers. . . .

And whereas by his Majesty's commission under the Great Seal of England, you are thereby ordered and empowered to make war upon the Mughal or Great King of Indostan, and his subjects, as you shall be directed by the East India Company and their chief officers in India aforesaid, we do therefore think it advisable and do hereby require you, that in case you meet with any of the Great Mughal's, or his subjects' ships in the sea in your passage to Bombay, that in such case you do require and compel them by force of arms or otherwise to go along with you to Bombay, to the intent that if our General and Governor of Bombay Sir John Child Baronet or any other of the Company's servants be forcibly detained at Surat, or elsewhere in the said king's dominions or the Company's goods or estates there, those Moors' ships may be detained, condemned and confiscated to the Company's use at Bombay, towards the satisfaction of those and other damages done formerly to the East India Company for which no reparation hath yet been made [to] them.

But until such condemnation be made of such ships or junks and their loadings, you are by no means to suffer any injury to be offered to the merchants, commanders or seamen of any such Moor's ship or vessel, nor the value of a penny to be taken from any person, or out of any such ship, as you will answer the contrary to our Sovereign Lord the King and to his Majesty's East India Company at your peril.

---

[6]Topass, or topaz, was a term often used to refer to Luso-Indian Christians, particularly soldiers. Canareen (Konkani) can have various meanings, but here it probably refers to fighters from the coastal areas south of Portuguese Goa. Rajputs were fighters from various states in north and western India.

11

BARTHOLOMEW HARRIS AND SAMUEL ANNESLEY

Diplomatic Overtures between Surat and the Company

1687

This letter, sent by two members of the Surat factory to Sir John Child, governor of Bombay and general over the East India Company's forces in India, was published as a pamphlet in England, presumably at the behest of the London directors of the Company, who wanted to deflect criticism of their war and show progress toward peace. The letter illuminates the informal character of diplomacy as well as the involvement of elite women in politics.

May it please Your Excellency &c.[1]

In our last we advised Your Excellency, &c. of Mukhtiar Khan [the mutasaddi of Surat] sending for Kishan and Vithal Parekh [the Company's brokers in Surat] who accordingly went from hence the 22th instant [i.e., in the current month] and the next day they met him in his way coming to Bardoly.[2] Upon his being acquainted with who they were, he immediately stopped his horse, and causing them to come near him, after they had made their obeisance [i.e., done the requisite homage], they presented him with five Soonaes[3] and nine Rupees which, having took, he spoke mighty kindly to them, telling them that he was come on purpose to make an end of our business, and if it pleased God he would speedily do it to all their contents. And after some such like discourse he proceeded [on his way].

---

[1] &c (i.e., et cetera, or etc.) refers to the rest of the governing council at Bombay.
[2] Bardoli was a pargana (or administrative and revenue division) near Surat.
[3] Gold pieces.

The True Copy of a Letter from Mr. Harris and Mr. Annesley, Two of the East India Company's Council left at Surat by their General Sir John Child, Baronet, when he and the rest of the English nation departed the Indian shore, and retired to Bombay, to begin the late War against the Great Mogul and his subjects (London, 1688), 1–5.

After [that] his Begum[4] with all her female attendants (who it seems concerns herself very much in her husband's and State affairs), being acquainted by her eunuch that our brokers were there, likewise made a stop, and calling them nearer (after they had made their present of fourteen Rupees and paid their respects) she told them she had understood our business, and she would take care of it, bidding them [to] send for the ships,[5] and so calling for some beetle[6] for them. The eunuch told her it was a great way behind, but she would not stir until they brought them some, which being given them, she likewise proceeded on her way.

When they were at Bardoly the Governor [i.e., the mutasaddi of Surat] sent for our brokers again, and discoursed with them a long time very kindly, giving them great protestations of his friendship to Your Excellency and our nation and having been pre-acquainted of our being here by Mirza Mosum Gelleeree[7] (at whose house Your Excellency lay when at Oorpaur,[8] where Kartalab Khan[9] gave Your Excellency a visit). He gave each of them a vest and ordered them to return so soon as possible to Surat, and bring us to him; and accordingly they travelled in the night, and came to us yesterday morning, and acquainted us with all the forgoing particulars, and of his kind invitation of us to him. After due consideration we resolved to go, and judging it unavoidable to go before him without some handsome present, and being un-provided with anything of our own growth, we procured a pair of pearl drops, to the value of four hundred Rupees, which we carried with us, and putting ourselves in the best equipage we could, we set out about noon, and arrived at the place where the Governor had pitched his tents about three o'clock, and had immediate admittance to him, where we were extraordinarily kindly received. . . .

We told him that Your Excellency had represented your grievances and desires to His Majesty [i.e., the Emperor Aurangzeb] in thirty-five articles[10] (which he pretended he had not seen, and so demanded them)

[4]A high-ranking woman; roughly translated to English as "Lady" or princess.

[5]She is presumably asking them to request John Child to return the ships his people had captured.

[6]Betel leaves, chewed as a stimulant and medicinal; often served wrapped around areca nuts.

[7]Mirza Mosum was one of the wealthier merchants at Surat; the Company often did business with him.

[8]Most likely Ulpar, a pargana under Surat's jurisdiction, which John Child had visited in 1683.

[9]Kartalab Khan had been mutasaddi at Surat and maintained a residence at Ulpar.

[10]Earlier, Child had issued a list of thirty-five "demands" to emissaries from Surat, which included the restoration of Company goods and reputation in Surat, the extradition of Englishmen in Surat who violated either Company or Mughal laws and

which . . . [if they were] granted Your Excellency &c. would be able to follow their merchandising and live peaceably in his county as formerly. . . . We motioned [i.e., proposed] the delivering up of Bowcher,[11] &c. to be delivered up to us to be sent down to Your Excellency, &c. which if he did, it would be a great inducement to Your Excellency, &c. to believe the reality of the King's and His Lordship's love towards us. . . .

And then [he] took Bartholemew Harris's hand in his and said, as he desired God's blessing on him and his, so truly would he see a true performance of those articles, which he took up in his other hand. And for a further proof of my sincerity (said he) I do here swear to the same by our Prophet Mohammed whom I worship and by Jesus Christ whom you adore that I will perform what I here say.

Further be pleased to consider the great weight of your Excellency's &c. Thirty Five Articles, that without Your Excellency's own person in this business it cannot be brought to that hopeful issue as may be desired.

[The pamphlet includes a postscript to the letter as follows:]

Some few days after receipt of the former letter the English General received another letter from the aforesaid two persons of his council, intimating that the said Prince or great lord Mukhtiar Khan was sending two envoys unto him to Bombay; for whom the General sent a noble barge or galley to bring them from the nearest part of the main-[land] to Bombay, and received them with the greatest honor and respect. They presented the General from the said Prince or Lord an exceeding courteous letter, inviting him to Swally[12] to put an end to all differences, which letter besides the said great Lord's chop (or common signature) had the print of his hand in saffron, which is the greatest assurance of honor and veracity that any prince in the East, of the Mahometan [i.e., Muslim] persuasion can make or give. The General received the letter with the customary ceremony to letters received from such great Princes, but told the envoys he was at present engaged in dispatching another ship for England, but he would consider of the peace proposed

---

of the Sidi's soldier who had killed the Englishmen at Bombay, and reduced customs at Surat; rights to mint coin; and many other conditions.

[11]George Bowcher, an English interloper and enemy of the Company, who had taken up residence at Surat and whom local officials there had been protecting.

[12]Swally (Suvali): The coastal town just to the west of Surat, which served as its main port and harbor.

and return a speedy answer, &c. So that upon the whole matter the East India Company do conclude, that there is an honorable conclusion made of that war, long since occasioned by the unnatural and pernicious attempts of interlopers, and that peace may continue between the Mughal and the Company, upon fair and just terms for as many ages as it did before, which was near a hundred years.

12

EAST INDIA COMPANY

Letter to the Mughal Emperor Aurangzeb
1688

In this official letter to the Mughal emperor, dated September 7, 1688, the London-based East India Company court of committees explains the reasons for hostilities that had begun in Bengal one year earlier. While insisting that it was Mughal officials' interference with English trade that was to blame for causing the war, the letter nonetheless reveals the ways in which the East India Company, like all the other European companies in Asia, acted in a diplomatic and martial as well as commercial capacity.

To the most renowned glorious & victorious
Emperor of Indostan & many other
Mighty kingdoms & countries famous
Over all the earth by the just & magnificent
Title of Mahomed Orang Zeib Sha Alemguir[1]

May it please your most Imperial Majesty
    We the ancient renowned English East India Company are not a little grieved that ever we should be necessitated to make use of our powerful

---

[1]That is, Mohammad Aurangzeb Shah Alamgir (1618–1707, r. 1658–1707). The Mughal emperor Aurangzeb was also known by his title Alamgir, or world-seizer. The original spelling is retained here for its historical value.

British Library, India Office Records E/3/91 fols. 291–92.

maritime force (which were always designed by us to serve your Royal Majesty and Empire) against your Majesty's innocent good natured subjects amongst whom we have lived and with whom we have had great commerce during the whole time of your Majesty's most illustrious fortunate reign, as well as in the happy reigns of your Majesty's glorious father[2] and grandfather[3] of immortal memory, in all which time, we dare appeal to all your Majesty's noble & righteous princes & governors and to all your honest Subjects whether we have not behaved ourselves peaceably and justly.

We hope your Majesty being moved by your renowned & unparalleled justice will give us leave on this occasion to say further that it is known to all your viziers [i.e., ministers] we have brought more wealth into your kingdom than all other European nations, one ship of ours carrying more money into your countries and making a more advantageous trade to your subjects than six ships of other nations.

What occasioned the breach and the late war was not any fault of ours nor of our chief servants, but the insupportable avarice and oppression of some of the meanest of your majesty's governors, who not having the fear of God before their eyes (as your Majesty always hath) did not pay that duty and reverence to your Majesty's most just & gracious commands as they ought to have done, neither would suffer our just complaints to approach your Majesty's most righteous throne.

As we are a people constantly affected to trade such was likewise the precipitate inclination of those that serve us in our chiefest trusts in India, which strong inclination to trade we have just cause to fear may have engaged them into a hasty peace without those requisite articles which were necessary to the conservation of it and are in truth as much for the advantage of your Majesty's subjects, as for the security of our servants' lives and of our estates within your Majesty's dominions.

Such an article is your Majesty granting to us some convenient healthful place in Bengal to fortify and defend our concerns from the insolence and wickedness of any of your Majesty's under-governors that may do injury or violence to our servants, or to our estates without your Majesty's leave or knowledge, as many of them did in Bengal to the forcing us to attempt that revenge which in honor and prudence we were bound to endeavor, though very much against the natural bent of our minds, which hath always been to pursue our commerce innocently and peaceably without affecting dominion, increase of territory, or the oppression

---

[2]Shah Jahan (r. 1628–1658).
[3]Jahangir (r. 1605–1627).

of other prince's subjects, which other European nations in India have manifestly practiced, but ourselves never.

It is very true your Imperial Majesty is graciously pleased to allow us Fort St. George [Madras] to inhabit as our free territory, which is as much as we shall ever desire on that coast with a little larger convenience for gardens and country refreshments. But that is not a place for harboring and repairing our ships, which is the ground of our humble petition to your Majesty for a place in Bengal, where we may harbor and repair our ships, if we should at any time be compelled into a war with any other European nation for the defense of your Majesty's subjects and their ships and trade at sea, for which purpose no European nation is better prepared, nor so conveniently situated as we are at our island of Bombay and there is no European nation that your Majesty's subjects have had more experience of nor will sooner trust than the faithful English nation, which either we shall always continue to deserve from your Majesty and all your good subjects, and therefore we humbly beseech your imperial Majesty to grant us such convenience with the liberty of coining what bullion we bring from Europe in such our fortified towns, that it may be always ready suddenly to give out to your Majesty's poor subjects to enable them to buy goods and make such manufactures as we have occasion of, the want of which liberty of coining rupees hath been a great hindrance to your Majesty's poor subjects and an insupportable prejudice to our trade in causing our ships to be kept so long in the Country for want of loading, as hath sometimes disabled them from returning home with safety.

All this we most humbly represent to your Imperial Majesty's most wise and pious consideration, praying your Majesty's full & gracious Farman for the purposes aforesaid, which will oblige us upon all occasions to adventure our treasure and strength in the defense of your Majesty's empire and of your subjects' ships and estates at sea against any opposition whatsoever and ever to remain.

Directions given touching the said letter: It is left to his Excellency [John Child] the general or president to affix the Company's seal (which is sent loose) unto the letter in such manner as is most usual in like cases which was not done here in regard [to] the nature of the embellishments required. That the same should be covered with white paper to prevent the tarnishing of them and after sealing to cover the same with cloth of gold or otherwise as may be most acceptable. A duplicate hereof is intended to be sent by the [ship] Kempthorne.

5

Other Experiences of the Siege

13

ALEXANDER HAMILTON

A More Critical View of the Siege
1689–1690

Alexander Hamilton was a Scottish trader and ship's captain who worked on and off for the East India Company but had become allied with "interlopers," that is, English and Scottish merchants who traded in violation of the East India Company's monopoly. As a sea captain, Hamilton was well-informed about the balance of power among the various groups at Bombay and coastal India, including the Sidis. Like James Hilton, Hamilton was an eyewitness to the siege, although he offers a quite different account of it. (See Hilton's diary, page 27.) Unlike Hilton, however, Hamilton published his version, albeit much later, in 1727, as part of a book that doubled as both a travel narrative and a critique of the East India Company's trade and government.

[Grievances over trade] were the foundation on which General Child built a war with the Mughal, without ever sending them [i.e., the grievances] to [the Mughal] Court to know the King's pleasure, but, without declaring war, seized his subject's ships wherever they were found, although they had the sanction of his [i.e., the emperor's] own passes. . . . [This war] cost his masters [i.e., the East India Company]

Alexander Hamilton, *A New Account of the East Indies, being the observations and remarks of Capt. Alexander Hamilton, who spent his time there from the year 1688 to 1723*, 2 Vols. (Edinburgh: John Mosman, 1727), vol. I: 213, 215–24, 227, 237, 240–41.

above £400,000 before they could lay it [i.e., end it], beside the loss of their credit with the Mughal and his subjects, which, to this time, is not quite recovered. . . .

On the General's passage [back] to Bombay [from Surat] he met with a fleet of vessels that were carrying corn [i.e., grain] to an army of the Mughal's that lay at Danda-Rajpuri,[1] about fourteen leagues to the southward of Bombay. That fleet he also seized and carried to Bombay, though against the opinion of most of his Council. Before this seizure he asked the opinion of some sea-officers, and one Captain Hilder, being the eldest, advised him not to meddle with the corn fleet, because it would straiten [i.e., cause hardship to] the army, and force them to look abroad for provisions, where it might best be procured, and perhaps might affect Bombay, which was in a great measure beholden to their neighbors for sustenance and firewood. The General took him [i.e., Hilder] up with scurrilous language, calling him coward and fool, and bragged that if Sidi Yakut (which was the Mughal's general's name) should dare to come with his forces on Bombay, he would blow him off again with the wind of his bum [i.e., by farting at him].

Cowards are generally stout when dangers arise at a distance and so was our General, who had never seen a sword drawn in anger, and consequently [was] very ill-acquainted with war. And when it came to his door, none was ever so confounded and dejected as he was, as appeared by his conduct in that war that he so foolishly brought on himself and his Country. . . .

When the news came to Sidi Yakut that his fleet with his provision of corn and cloth were seized and carried to Bombay, he sent a civil letter to our General [requesting him] to discharge his fleet, protesting that, as he had not meddled in the affairs between him and the Suraters [i.e., people from the city of Surat], he would continue neuter [i.e., neutral] unless he was forced to do otherwise. But our General gave him an insolent answer and the fleet was unladed [i.e., unloaded] at Bombay.

Sidi Yakut sent again to desire the delivery of his fleet in fair terms, otherwise he would be obliged to come with his army and quarter on Bombay where his provisions were detained, and that if his fleet was not set at liberty before the 11th of February, which was near at hand, he would certainly be on Bombay the 14th. But still receiving uncivil answers he performed his promise to a tittle [i.e., to a T], for that very night he landed at a place called Sewri (about four miles distant from the main Fort) with 20,000 men at his back.

[1]Sidi Yakut had his stronghold at Danda-Rajpuri.

Our General's [sense of] security had made him neglect providing for receiving such guests, trusting to the reputation of his forces, who were greater then than ever they had been before, or ever were since that time. And he had small ships enough, had they been placed in proper places, that might certainly have hindered his [i.e., the Sidi's] landing and forced him home again. But all those necessary preparations were neglected and the Sidi landed at midnight, and the redoubt where he landed fired a great gun to give the alarm, and so deserted their post, and the Sidi took possession of it. At 1:00 in the morning the Castle fired three guns to give the general alarm, which brought such fear on those that lived securely in their houses without [i.e., outside] the Castle that the poor ladies, both white and black, run half-naked to the Fort and only carried their children with them. But they were all obliged to wait without the wall till daylight relieved them.[2] . . .

The following day some of the Enemy appeared on Mazagaon Hills which grieved our General's righteous soul to see infidels come so near him in a hostile manner. He called a minion of his own, one Captain Paine who was no better soldier than himself, and ordered him to take two companies, each containing about seventy men, and march to those hills and drive the Enemy out of his sight. He ordered one Monroe, who had been a soldier at Tangier, to be his lieutenant. In Tangier he [i.e., Monroe] had received a wound in his heel that spoiled his running, and accordingly they marched in good order within shot of the Enemy, who showed their heads above the surface of the hill but did not offer to advance or expose their bodies. Several gentlemen volunteers took their arms and accompanied the little army.

The lieutenant advised the captain to march up the hill in platoons to separate the Enemy's forces. The captain took it as an affront to be advised [and] told his lieutenant that when he had the command in his own hands he might use it as he thought fit, but as it was entrusted to him he would use it according to his own mind, and so ordered his men to spread [out] as much as they could, and when they saw the Enemy open in the plain to discharge [their guns] all at once amongst them, which, he said, would terrify them. Monroe opposed his scheme and told him of the danger he would bring himself and them into if the Enemy should attack them whilst their arms were reloading. But nothing could dissuade him [i.e., Paine] from his project, and so commanded his men to fire as he had directed. The Sidis being ten to one in numbers

---

[2] The implication is that the General was too cowardly to open the gates even to save women and children.

and better runners than our men, and better acquainted with close fighting with sword and target [i.e., shield], took hold of the opportunity and advanced with all their speed, which the Captain perceiving, betook himself to his heels, and was the foremost man to the Portuguese [Catholic] Church, where he took courage to look behind him to see what was become of his men. Poor Monroe, thinking to stop the Enemy's career by a part of the wing that he commanded, found himself deserted by all but thirteen or fourteen stout fellows, who were soon surrounded by the Enemy and cut to pieces.

Paine had not stopped at the Portuguese Church had he not found a party of a hundred men that lay there ready to support or receive him as his case should require. He was a fellow as well made for running as any I ever saw, and was so much in the General's favor that he had not so much as a reprimand for his cowardice and misbehavior. This relation I had from a gentleman volunteer who kept always near the Captain while he could keep pace with him. . . .

And now the Sidi being master of the whole island except the Castle and about half a mile to the southward of the Castle, he raised batteries on Dungaree [Dongri] Hill, which overlooked the Fort wall, and disturbed the garrison very much. Then he put four great guns in the Custom House, commonly called the India House, and raised a battery at the Moody's House, within 200 paces of the Fort, and another in the lady's house that he [i.e., Governor Child] had been so unkind to,[3] so that it was dangerous to go out or in at the Castle gate, till we got up a half moon [i.e., a semi-circular barricade] before it. All men were then pressed into the Company's service, and I amongst the rest. We passed the months from April to September very ill, for provisions grew scarce by the addition of 3,000 Sevajees[4] that were employed as auxiliaries in the military service of the Company. . . .

The ill success we had ashore with the Enemy made our General sick, and in December he dispatched two factors to the Mughal's court with a Surat merchant called Mir Nazim. He was our friend and had some interest [i.e., influence] at Court. They went under the name of[5] the English ambassadors. Mr. George Weldon was first in commission and Abraham Navarro, a Jew, was second. In fifteen Days they arrived

---

[3]The widow of John Thorburn, who had supported a widespread mutiny of soldiers and civilians—which came to be known as Keigwin's Rebellion—at Bombay in 1683. Child is said to have evicted her from her home after her husband had died in prison.

[4]Other sources suggest there were about 2,000 Maratha troops.

[5]Hamilton here is dismissively implying they were not real ambassadors but mere commercial emissaries.

at Court, being then at Jehanabant. They were received but coldly, but about the middle of April, by the special assistance of presents to the officers at Court, they were admitted to audience, but were brought to Aurangzeb's presence after a new mode for ambassadors, their hands being tied by a sash before them, and were obliged to prostrate. The King gave them a severe reprimand and then asked their demands. They first made a confession of their faults and desired pardon, then that their farman which was forfeited should be renewed, and the Sidi and his army should be ordered off Bombay. . . . [D]uring the war, about sixty Europeans of several nations had deserted from us and took pay of the Sidi. The reason they gave for their desertion was ill usage they had received from some Irish officers, yet most of them returned after the war, on promise of pardon.

The farman being ready, and the required security given, Sidi Yakut left Bombay the 8th of June, 1690. But he also left a pestilence behind him which in four months' time destroyed more men than the war had done, and for joy [the Sidi] made a malicious bonfire of his headquarters, Mazagaon Fort. . . .

And of seven or eight hundred English that inhabited [Bombay] before the war, there were not above sixty left by the sword and plague, and Bombay, that was one of the pleasantest places in India, was brought to be one of the most dismal deserts. . . .

Danda-Rajpuri lies seven leagues to the southward of Chaul.[6] [It is] a town belonging to the Sidi, who generally lies there with a fleet of the Mughal's vessels and ships of war, and an army of thirty or forty thousand men. This place affords a good harbor for his fleet and the country about feeds good numbers of black cattle, from whence Bombay is mostly supplied when they keep in good terms with the Sidi. Otherwise he makes them feed on fish, which that Island [Bombay] is plentifully stored with; but now worse than before the Sidi's War.

[6]Chaul was a Portuguese stronghold in the Province of the North, located to the south of Bombay.

14

THE GOVERNOR AND COUNCIL OF BOMBAY

Letter to London about the Siege

1689

This letter and the deposition that follows (Document 15) are linked documents. The first is part of a routine correspondence between the Bombay council and the Company's governing court of committees in London. In the letter, Bombay's leadership describes the hardships the island was facing as a result of the siege, stressing in particular the difficulty the East India Company had maintaining effective discipline in its garrison.

Bombay Council to London (Dec. 26, 1689)

We have since their departure[1] used all diligence and our utmost endeavors to beat the enemy off the island, but in vain for he daily encroaches upon us and is now very near us and builds strong batteries, so that hourly shots pass between both parties, [though] not, we thank God, in the least to dismay us, and the enemy is very sensible we are not to be frightened. He has felt the force of our arms and finds that his numbers cannot conquer a handful of us, but he has been soundly banged and we killed abundance of his multitudes, but he as fast fills them up again, whilst we cannot repair our losses, which make us the more sparing of our countrymen.

It is true we must confess it is a great evil that our own garrison soldiers should desert us and not only that but in actual arms against us, and one of them is worse to us than 100 of the black enemies. We have killed a great many of them but too many [are] still alive against us. For Your Honor's satisfaction we now send the depositions of one [who] ran lately away from the enemy to us. We have had many came over to us but none under the same circumstances that turned Mahometan [i.e., Muslim]. He is a young foolish fellow and we believe was more afraid

---

[1] That is, the departure of two East India Company ships, the *Charles II* and *London*, for England in June of that year.

British Library, India Office Records E/3/48 fol. 99.

than hurt, which made him turn. But we do not think the enemy so very base as to have killed him [even if he had not converted]. Besides they are under a dread that we should certainly put to death all we catch of theirs and we have a great many now in irons working in the fort, and certainly should they do that [i.e., start killing their prisoners] for every one of our countrymen [who dies] we would sacrifice 100 of theirs, and truly it would put us into too great a passion to spare any that fell into our hands.

The black people we entertained in your Honor's service behave not themselves as we could wish, [though] they are indeed as good as the enemy's [forces]. But we cannot expect 2,000 should fight with 14,000 of the same color and we really believe they [i.e., our enemies] have more [than 14,000 men on the island]. We even repent we ever entertained the rascals.[2] They have indeed put you to a great charge thereby but we thought we did [it] for the best. We are now 4 months pay behindhand with them and they do us some kindness being on the out guards. And because we are in some hopes of coming to an accommodation with the Mughal [emperor] and [expect] to hear suddenly how affairs are like to go, [we] do wait with patience and forbear. [B]ut if things go not according to expectation [we] shall think of some other way, and we with the help of God will keep the Fort and never part with it whilst we have any men to stand by us.

But indeed it is hard with us. We have but few of our countrymen, as your Honors will see by the [muster] rolls now sent, and our unhappiness is much the greater because of reports given out by the Dutch, French, Portuguese and indeed also all over India concerning our native country.[3] And it's an addition to our unhappiness because we have [had] no ship this year from your Honors nor never a one at Fort St. George [Madras] [since] the 14th September last as we understand. But all was in peace and quietness there thank God and they not at all disturbed which we are heartily glad of and hope they will continue in peace and not be put to those shifts and troubles we have had and still are in.

---

[2]The council is presumably referring here to the Maratha troops.
[3]This is a reference to rumors circulating but not yet confirmed in Bombay about the Revolution of 1688–89.

15

JOHN STEVENS, ALIAS ABD AL-ALLAH

Conversion to Islam while at the Sidi's Camp

1689

This deposition of John Stevens, a Company soldier who had deserted to or perhaps been captured by the Sidis, was taken down by Company officials at Bombay upon his attempt to return to the garrison and was included as an enclosure with the foregoing letter (Document 14). Stevens, who also had taken the name Abd al-Allah while in the Sidi's service, mounts a different kind of plea from the letter. It is difficult to know whether Stevens was originally a deserter or a prisoner of war, though he labors to prove that he was the latter. The council's cover letter treats him as something between the two, since he had clearly drawn pay from the Sidi and taken up arms against his countrymen (generally a capital offense in wartime). Taking down depositions was a common practice in Company governance, and Stevens took advantage of this opportunity to plead his case, both for converting and, less directly, for taking up arms for the Sidi. His is the fullest known description in English of the Sidi's camp, and it also contains additional information about Sidi Yakut himself.

Bombay Castle December 21st 1689

The Deposition of John Stevens (alias Abd al-Allah since circumcised) who this day about 11 o'clock ran from the Sidi's battery at Lieutenant Nangle's to our battery at the Moody's House and was at the same time brought into the Fort before the worshipful deputy governor and declared as follows:

Declares that, belonging to the yacht Josiah and being on the 7th August 1689 passed at night in a gallevat lying at anchor by Cross Island, there came out two boats of the Sidi's from Mazagaon. Since [it was] understood [the boats] designed to steal guns if [they] could out of either the battery ships or the bunder [i.e., warehouse and pier] . . . one Ward in

British Library, India Office Records E/3/48 fol. 91–92.

the gallevat called to them in Moorish[1] and bid them come to us. They answered they would not, on which Ward ordered our people to fire at them, which going to do, several muskets snapped in [the] pan[2] and would not go off, [all] except one blunderbuss[3] and a musket or two. Thereupon we flung a grenade shell into one of the boats, but the fire went out so it did no execution, on which they came [even] with us and flung in several baskets of stones in to us, upon which the coolies[4] (all but two) leaped over board. We stood still on our defense but finding them to overpower us, one Charles Jones and myself leapt over board and swam to Cross Island where [we] met with the coolies that had leapt over board before. It was about 11 a clock at night when we came on the island and [we] continued [there] till the next day at 12 or one. At noon when came off to us from Mazagaon one of the Sidi's boats which took the coolies off and we endeavoring to swim towards the yacht but were soon overtaken by the boat that seized us and so carried us to Mazagaon before the Sidi himself who was then there. When we came before him, [he] bid us not [to] fear but be of good courage and so sent us up by the catwall [kotwal or commandant] to be put into stocks where we lay three days and nights, then were afterwards taken out and chained together as were all besides of our gallevat. . . . [For] fifteen days we were fed in prison and irons with less and less daily and word [was] sent to us by the Sidi that if we would not turn Moor [i.e., convert to Islam] he would starve us to death or cut off our heads, upon which seven of us did consent to turn Moor, then was presently circumcised. Our names vizt [being as follows], John Hopton, John Farmer, Robert Perkins, Charles Jones, Robert Simons, Richard Dingle and John Stevens, the deponent. After this [they] entered us into pay as soldiers at 14 X[eraphins][5] per month, only Dingle and the deponent [Stevens got] 10 rupees per month, [the Sidi] also giving us victuals daily from his kitchen.

[1]It is hard to say precisely to what language he is referring, though possibly he means Hindustani.

[2]Said of a flintlock or snaplock musket (and later of other firearms) when the flint or snap fails to ignite the powder in the pan or ignites it without setting off the main charge.

[3]A short-barreled, large-caliber firearm with a flared muzzle, often used on board ships.

[4]"Coolies" refers both to workers generally and to the kolis, a caste often employed as laborers or servants, specifically.

[5]A unit of currency, common on the west coast of India, equaling 3/5 rupee, and (at this time) about 1 shilling, 6–8 pence.

[The deponent, Stevens] declares that at Mazagaon is made a platform below our small fort[6] where is 4 guns of about 18 [and] 20 weight[7] and that the Sidi hath several boats and vessels comes with provisions and ammunition etc. to him from Surat, Underi[8] and Danda-Rajpuri, some [boats] coming into Mahim from Surat creeping in close by the shore, other[s] from the southward comes in betwixt Cross Island and Dongri[9] Battery. As to the quantity of men the Sidi hath on the island for fighting [Stevens] can [in] no ways [say] but hath heard the Sidi say (when any of our people in drink have troubled him) that he had 14,000 fighting men on this island up and down, which was not so much trouble to him as the drunken Europeans. [This deponent, Stevens] declares the Sidis are very populous [i.e., numerous] and as to the strength they have hereabouts at Dongri Battery [and other] batteries, they have small guns but how many [he] knows not and the largest of all [is] at Nangle's Battery. The batteries [are] all full of men but how many in each [he] knows not. Two thirds of his [the Sidi's] fighting men [are] Hindus [such] as Rajputs, etc. [Stevens] declares it's reported the Sidi hath about 3 [or] 4000 fighting men at Mahim; [what number] at Sion and Veroly[10] he knows not, and few reported to be at Sewri Bay. [Stevens] declares the Sidi hath made a trench from Nangle's Battery to the pillory (through which he made his escape) about 8 [or] 9 foot deep and 18 [or] 20 foot broad. [Stevens] declares that about six weeks ago [some] bombs were played from hence [i.e., from the fort] upon the Sidi's people at Nangle's house, which killed at one time four men and wounded others; at another time killed two men and a boy and wounded more. [He] declares our great shot have done several mischiefs which [he] cannot remember too particular, but remarkable that two double headed shot came just over the Sidi's head as he lay on his cot (which much feared him) in the Portuguese Church which caused him to alter his apartment there [i.e., to bunk somewhere else].

[Stevens] declares that in the last field fight but one John Johnson, a Dutchman, was wounded through both thighs at two several [i.e., separate] times and yesterday died; [during the same altercation] one Thomas Parrell was shot through the hip, and now lies sick still of his

---

[6]A fort built by the English but now occupied by the Sidi's forces.

[7]That shot eighteen- or twenty-pound shot.

[8]Underi was a small island in the Bombay outer harbor that the Sidi had seized and fortified in 1680.

[9]"Dungaree" in original.

[10]This is probably Worli.

wound; one Gerard, a Dutchman was also at the same time wounded in the thigh but recovered it.[11] [Stevens] declares that the following persons . . . [have] turned Mahometans: Jonathan Servell, Evert Evertson, James Graves, John Powell, John Marding, Richard Reardiworth, Matthew Empson, John Scott, Edward Dawson, John Carter, James Merriday, Thomas Sinjan, John Green, Thomas Corey, Clement George, Cobut (a Dutchman), Charles Lacy, Thomas Neale, John Yates, Oliver Nickson, James Patson [and others] not at present in [his] memory [i.e., he cannot remember their names]. [He] declares the Sidi hath now with him above sixty Europeans of his guard most [of them] Englishmen . . . [and] has great intentions of mining to our church and the new battery at Thornburn's house. They have begun already [to dig the trench] but find the water as they dig to hinder their proceedings. . . .

[He] declares the Sidi is very hot in his expectations to gain the great tomb at Mendham's Point[12] which if [he] can effect [it he intends] there to fortify, to prevent our boats from landing in the Bay etc.[13] [Stevens] declares the Portuguese at Bandora assist the Sidi much. [He] declares the Padre Superior at Bandora have been several times with the Sidi and [there is] a daily correspondence betwixt them. [He] declares that there is many of the shroffs,[14] banians[15] and so on that formerly belonged to us [that are now] with the Sidi and a Portuguese scrivan [i.e., scribe] Manuell. [Stevens] declares there is a continual correspondence betwixt the Sidi and some of these country people that belong to us, [and] that [they] daily advise the Sidi [of] all actions and transactions that is done here in the Fort etc. [He] declares that when the white flag was [i.e., is] put out at Nangle's Battery it was reported [that] 200 Sivajis [i.e., Maratha fighters] of ours were to come over [i.e., desert] to [the] Sidi's [side]. [Stevens] declares that the Sidi sayeth that he hath no intentions of storming the fort should he stay here seven[ty] and seven year[s], for the King and some particular merchants maintain him and his army. [Stevens] declares finally that thus he made his escape: the Sidi coming today from Mazagaon to the Portuguese Church, he took up his musket and bandoleers and came to

---

[11]All of these were Europeans fighting for the Sidi.

[12]A spot at the southern tip of Bombay, which housed English, Jewish, and Muslim burial grounds.

[13]Control of Mendham's Point would have allowed the Sidi to rake the entrance to the harbor with cannon fire.

[14]Bankers and money-changers.

[15]Banians: Hindu merchants (see Document 1).

Nangle's Battery where some Pathans ordered him to charge his petre[16] and be ready to fire when commanded, [to] which [he] said he would, but told them [he] must go to ease himself so [went back] through the trench as before mentioned. . . . He said that threats and the fear of death made him turn Moor and was circumcised as before mentioned but hopes for your Excellency's favorable [word unreadable] towards him and candor to him.

[16]Presumably to load or prime his firearm.

6

The Quest for Peace

16

THE COMPANY'S RESPONSE TO MUKHTIAR KHAN

A Peace Proposal from Surat

1689

In April 1689, Mukhtiar Khan, the mutasaddi (head of the port) of Surat, sent word to Sir John Child, via the head Jesuit priest at Bandora, setting out the conditions under which he would agree to start peace negotiations. (The Portuguese had offered to serve as intermediary in the conflict as well as to use their territory as neutral ground on which to conduct the negotiations.) Mukhtiar Khan proposed four main prerequisites for talks: (1) that Sir John Child, the Company's General, go personally to Portuguese Damão to negotiate; (2) that the two leaders would meet there, with the Portuguese Captain of the North acting as mediator; (3) that these talks take place before Sidi Yakut vacated the island, and that Child and the English negotiators come only if they had power to negotiate in the name of the English king; and (4) that the Company return the ships and goods that had been seized from the Surat merchants. These propositions coming only a few months after the Sidi's invasion, Child and the rest of the council were still not disposed toward any sort of compromise and remained convinced (not without reason) that the demand that Child attend in person was a ruse to get him imprisoned or killed. The following document contains the Bombay council's responses to Mukhtiar Khan's overtures.

Proposals made by Mukhtiar Khan to Bombay, April 27, 1689, British Library, India Office Records E/3/48 fols. 7–8.

1st

This unanimously declared by the General and the whole body of English in council with him that they are ready for peace with the Mughal [and] his Subjects and it cannot be thought otherwise by any [person of] sense and reason, if they will but look back and consider that the English General went twice up to Surat in order to make the peace, and there delivered up to Mukhtiar Khan several ships with their ladings and vessels laden with corn, and this [is] notoriously known to the world. Now it is expected that the English General should go to Damão to treat with the same person that has so often deceived him. 'Tis late in the year [so that] by sea he cannot go with any safety, and to pass through the Portuguese country by land it is not safe for his person, and very dangerous because of the faithlessness of the Moors and the great forces they have about their country.[1] . . . [I]t is fit for us to be thoroughly satisfied with [the] security the Portuguese can give for the General's safe return to the Castle of Bombay, but it will be much better if some other persons [duly?] commissioned might go up to Damão and conclude this one after with the Nabob [i.e., Mukhtiar Khan].[2]

2d

This is answered in the preceding article but a little it may be argued that the Nabob is but Governor of the town, whereas the English General represents the whole nation. And further the Governor of Surat came not where he is on account of making peace but by his king's order to prosecute the war against us.

3d

As to what place may be appointed by the Captain General &c for the secure treating [i.e., negotiating for peace] with the Nabob, we are willing with him to leave that to the discretion of the Captain General and Portuguese gentlemen, but in this we are plain and positive, and it cannot be thought otherwise [than] reasonable, and fair by all understanding persons that the Sidi [Yakut] must with all his forces leave the Island [of] Bombay before any of the English of quality can set forth hence for

[1] It is not clear if "Moors" here refers to the Sidi's forces specifically or to Mughal forces more generally.

[2] This appears to mean: it is reasonable for us to demand complete satisfaction with respect to the security arrangements, and since we are not likely to be satisfied, a person of lower status should go.

Damão to treat with that Nabob. And for the satisfaction of the Nabob himself and for the Captain General &c [Gentlemen] mediators in this affair we are willing he give under our hands in the name of our most serene and great king, that on our parts we will not be wanting on reason, honorable and fair [warrants] to make a firm peace, and are ready now as we always were to receive the Mughal's farman that is now in Mukhtiar Khan's hands with all due honor and respect as becomes us to so great [a] king.

4th

To this article we wholly agree provided we may do it with that security as to have the king's farman to pay 2 percent custom at Surat and no more, and our demands formerly delivered [to] Mukhtiar Khan complied with all and to have free trade in all the Mughal's dominions and enjoy all our ancient privileges in all parts of his dominions without being imposed upon by any of his governors.

17

Peace Negotiations between the Company and the Mughals

July 1689 to February 1690

In May 1689, Governor John Child selected three peace envoys, George Weldon, Barker Hibbins, and Abraham Navarro, all East India Company employees, to negotiate a settlement with envoys from Surat at the Portuguese colony of Damão. The envoys for the other side, presumably selected by the governor of Surat, were Qazi Ibrahim, a sharia court judge, and Mir Nazim, a well-connected merchant. Weldon, Navarro, and Mir Nazim subsequently traveled to Aurangzeb's court, which was itself moving on a campaign through southern India. Though this account is narrated from the English point of view, the excerpts here nevertheless contain some fairly candid statements from the delegates

British Library, Sloane MSS 1910.

from Surat about what they thought of the behavior of the Company in general and of John Child in particular.

The Negotiations at Damão

July 23, 1689

Amongst the discourse we had this afternoon we told Qazi Ibrahim and Mir Nazim that we were free to deliver up all the ships, money and goods we had taken, excepting what [was] burnt and robbed by the Sidi, which we would in no way be answerable for, but that they must go to him for satisfaction. Further it was not their [bad] fortune alone. We had lost abundance of our own goods and the other damages done [to] Bombay would not be repaired these 20 years. To this Mir Nazim answered this was not the way to make peace, for all the merchants did expect full satisfaction for all damages received by us, and how could we expect the King would ever give us a farman unless he was fully satisfied by a writing under all the merchants' hands [i.e., signatures] [saying] that we had contented them [i.e., satisfied their demands for recompense]? As for the Sidi's coming upon the Island it was our own faults and none of theirs, for we drew them on ourselves to revenge the great affront done the King (i.e., the emperor Aurangzeb) by our taking his corn fleet. Therefore since so great a harm had been done by him, as we were the occasion, we ought to be the sufferers, and not them.[1] . . .

August 14, 1689

[W]e related to them what the General &c [i.e., the Bombay council] had wrote us, in answer to what had passed between us and them, which the General &c was positive to, and unless they could fully comply therewith, they could not expect any success in this treaty. They said if we stood [u]pon such hard terms there would be no peace and wars must go on, for we must not think to impose upon the King and bring him to our conditions, for what we had in our hands of the merchant[s] was no loss to him, and had we ten times as much, whether of his own, or belonging to other people, he would not value the loss of it, where it stood in competition with his honor. If we had forces to beat the Sidi

---

[1]The Company set in motion the events that led to the siege, so any damage they have incurred is their own fault.

off the Island, he could soon pour a greater number on [i.e., send more troops], which we might be sure to expect in two months' time.

After this Mir Nazim and Qazi Ibrahim were for going to Surat the next morning for they were satisfied (since the General &c had not complied with their offers, but rejected all and stood upon such high punctilios)[2] the General &c had no desire for peace, but only to get what they could and march off, for they thought they had offered everything fair, that any one that desired peace would have been glad to have embraced such an opportunity before matters had come to the extremity.[3]

We considered that the General did not know at their writing [that] the Nabob was turned out,[4] and that should this treaty be broke off, we did not know when another would begin, whether ever or no, and that this was an opportunity for the good of all not to be slighted. For should these men return again to Surat in the height of anger, what with the shame of their ill success and the scoff [that] would be put on them,[5] they would certainly represent us so ill, every way in all respects, both at Court and amongst their friends, that hereafter none would concern themselves any more about us, unless to forward our ruin. And that black character we have been represented in at Court by our enemies would stand so firmly against us that there would be no removing it, but by our removal out of India, and our poor countrymen at Surat would be used more like dogs than ever.[6]

These considerations made us think of some means to stay them, so we proposed it to them either to stay at Damão till we could have answer to another letter, or else for all of us to go to Bassein (from where a letter might go to Bombay in one day's time and an answer returned the next). They were very averse to it, and said it would signify nothing, but being well satisfied what our intentions drove at, we told them that another letter might effect something since the Nabob [Mukhtiar Khan] was turned out, for the General &c did never believe he was any ways real in his intentions, therefore now was the time. The Captain General &c joined with us in persuading them to it, telling them by their going thither [i.e., to Bassein], the world would see they were desirous

---

[2]Here the negotiators are referring to the fact that Child refused to negotiate directly with the mutasaddi (see the Company's response to Mukhtiar Khan, Document 16).

[3]Before the negotiations broke down completely.

[4]A few days earlier, news had come that the mutasaddi of Surat, Mukhtiar Khan, whom the Company considered to be an enemy, was being replaced.

[5]Scorn would be poured upon the Surat negotiators for having failed to reach an agreement.

[6]Some East India Company employees at Surat had been put under arrest by town officials.

of making peace, as well as we. So at last they were persuaded to it, and it was agreed we should go to Bassein together, leave them there, and we go to Bombay to represent the whole affair to the General and know their last resolutions whether for war or peace. . . .

September 20, 1689

We Sir John Child, General, John Vauxe, Geo[rge] Cook, Geo[rge] Weldon, English, do consent in the name of the Right Honorable Company to deliver up all whatsoever ships, goods and moneys belonging to the Surat, Broach, and Cambay Merchants as the account under mentioned shows, being the account of what [was] taken by us out of 21 Ships and in case of mortality or absence of any one, then the remaining persons stand bound to see this agreement fulfilled.

We are in expectation the King [i.e., the emperor Aurangzeb] will be pleased to forget whatsoever we have been faulty in, and give order [to] Sidi Yakut Khan to depart our Island of Bombay and order the Governor of Surat to set free our Englishmen and brokers from prison, whatever goods and moneys hath been seized on in Surat or elsewhere belonging to us to be delivered up, also to favor us in granting a farman in the name of the English Nation in the place of that given last year in the name of the General. And the 35 articles formerly presented to be answered in the same manner as before, and then we have free liberty to trade in all the dominions of the King with that freedom as we have desired, which shall make us pray for the King's health.

After this is all done, and we have delivered to the merchants what [is] in our hands belonging to them, we shall send our people to Surat and then make a present to the King of the value of one hundred thousand Rupees.

[There follows a list of ships and goods taken along with their assessed value, which are to be returned to their owners or for which recompense will be paid.]

We Sir John Child General, John Vauxe, George Cook and George Weldon, English, do consent and agree in the name of the R[ight] H[onorable] Company to give unto Ruila Khan (for [whom] Mir Nazim is security) 25,000 Rupees in ready money, when Sidi Yakut Khan is departed the Island, a farman come, our Englishmen and brokers cleared, and our monies and goods seized at Surat delivered to us. The like to be given to Mir Nazim on the same account. . . .

Journey to the Imperial Camp to Plead for Peace

Wednesday, November 27, 1689[7]

We set out from Bombay about three-o-clock in the afternoon with the manchua and two gallevats and arrived Thana about ten at night. It being too late to go on shore we remained on board.

Saturday, December 1, 1689

We arrived Kalyan betimes in the morning when [we] went on shore, landed our lumber [i.e., luggage] and carried all up to a small grove of trees by a large tank where [we] took up our quarters. . . . This town is a ruinated place [and] meanly inhabited having suffered very much by the long wars between Sivaji Rajah and the Mughal. The weights measures and coins [are] the same current in the Mughal's dominions which is one mark of his sovereignty and extends through all his conquests. . . .

Wednesday, December 4, 1689

The diwan[8] sent an officer to complain to us that notwithstanding the treaty we were upon, our boats went and robbed in the territories of his Master [the Mughal emperor] which at this time looked so unhandsome that should he advise the King of it [it] might at this juncture enrage him, and do our affairs great prejudice. But because he would not have a hand in spoiling what had [been] so long labored for, he would connive at it for this time [i.e., keep quiet about it for now], but withal desired us to make his resentments known to the General &c that a stop might be put to all such proceedings, which we did immediately. . . .

Saturday, December 14, 1689

We traveled up Vage Mack Ghat,[9] meeting with a very ill and dangerous passage which we overcame by the evening, and quartered ourselves by a tankside upon the ghat. But our lumber could not get up above half way, so were forced to sleep with empty stomachs, no victuals being

---

[7]The first page of the manuscript is erroneously dated 1688; the events clearly occurred in late 1689. The two parts of the diary are also misleadingly bound in reverse chronological order.

[8]A provincial imperial revenue collector and administrator, and often a quite powerful Mughal official.

[9]One of the major mountain passes into the Deccan.

procurable. One of our lustiest [i.e., strongest] of our Bandareens died at the foot of the ghat. . . .

Tuesday, December 17, 1689

We traveled 10 kos, the way very good, and came to a town called Umra which was welcome to us, for here we got victuals, having suffered hunger two days. Just when it was dark Mir Nazim's servant and our two Bandareens came back from Asad Khan[10] with a letter to Mir Nazim acquainting him that so soon as he had received his letter he showed it to the King, who seemed pleased with it and ordered him to give us quarter near him, and when we came to discourse us [i.e., to present our case] . . . he would make a report thereof to the King and then we should have admittance [i.e., we would be allowed to have an audience with the emperor]. . . .

Thursday, December 19, 1689

Being near the [Mughal] Camp we set out betimes leaving our lumber to follow and arrived there about eleven a clock, where we understood [the King] and most of his Omrahs [i.e., high court officials] had [marched] away 3 kos further this morning. . . . Mir Nazim advised us it was very dangerous to keep such a sum of money by us as we had brought, robberies being very frequent in the Army. Therefore [he] thought it much more secure to dispose it into the hand of a shroff, from whence we might draw it as occasion offered, which advice we thought not fit to be slighted, it being very insecure travelling with it in our palanquins amidst the army. . . . [We] therefore concluded to put it into the hands of one Underjee a shroff of good note belonging to Uollupadas and recommended to us by Mir Nazim, which was accordingly performed. The same shroff informed us that the Sidi had advised the English were desirous of making peace (being sorry for what they had done) and desired to know his order, to which answer was returned [that] what the English had done was forgiven them, provided they satisfied I'timad Khan and the merchants, and sent up two English men to Court, which was expected. We understand the Dutch Ambassador Johannes Bacherus is [there at court], but hath done his business very well, what with his great brags of destroying the English and sweeping the seas clear of them, and large presents. [All] together he [Bacherus] had a retinue of about 300 men. Our journey this day was ten or eleven kos. . . .

---

[10]Assett Ckaune in original; Aurangzeb's chief wazir, or minister.

Saturday, December 21, 1689

. . . In the Evening, we had [a] meeting with Nabob Asad Khan and Hakim Mahmud Zaid his pisdash,[11] to each of whom as usual we gave [a] small present. The Nabob did us the honor to receive us in a little place made up in his tent door, and discoursed us standing.[12] He told us the King had been very angry with us, but now he had undertaken our business, wherefore we might set our hearts at rest; it should have a good conclusion. We told him we did not question it, since so worthy a gentleman had undertaken it. He enquired our names, and then dismissed us. Mir Nazim at the same time delivered him the Governor of Surat's petition to the King in our behalfs, the agreement signed and sealed by the General and Council, and the General's petition to the King, all [of] which were to be delivered [to] the King this night. *[Diary breaks off here.]*

[11]Likely an inadvertent transposition of peshkar, "deputy."
[12]Talked to us standing up (a mark of respect).

18

THE EMPEROR AURANGZEB

Declaring a Peace? The Imperial Farman
1690

Weldon and Navarro's agreement seemed to achieve the East India Company's goals: a farman guaranteeing the Company's commercial and political rights in Mughal territories. Mughal officials continued to insist that John Child receive this grant personally at Surat, but, unbeknown to them, he had already died on February 4. His successor, Deputy Governor John Vauxe, traveled in his stead, though fully aware of the possibility that this would prove to be a trap. Vauxe received the farman with great fanfare on April 4. However, upon having it translated back at the factory, he and the others discovered that its terms were not remotely those upon

British Library, India Office Records E/3/48 fol. 156; British Library, Add.MS. 22,185, fol. 10.

which they thought they had agreed. Making matters worse, the text of the farman somehow made its way back to England, where the Company's enemies had it published to further their own cause of having the Company reformed or disbanded.

All the English having made a most humble submissive petition that the ill crimes they have done may be pardoned, and requested a noble farman to make their being forgiven manifest, and sent their vakils[1] to the Heavenly Palace the most illustrious in the world to get the Royal Favor. And I'timad Khan the Governor [i.e., mutasaddi] of Surat's Petition to the famous court equal to the skies, being arrived, that they would present the great King with a fine of 150,000 rupees to his most noble treasury resembling the sun and would restore the merchant's goods they took away to the owners of them, and would walk by the ancient customs of the port, and behave themselves for the future no more in such a shameful manner.

Therefore[2] his Majesty according to his daily favor to all the people of the world, hath pardoned their faults, mercifully forgiven them, and out of his princely condescension agrees that the present be put into the treasury of the port, the merchant's goods be returned, the Town flourish, and they follow their trade as in former times, and Mr. Child who did the disgrace be turned out and expelled. This order is irreversible.

---

[1]Vakil here refers to a representative or agent at the Mughal court.
[2]"Whereupon" and "wherefore," in other versions.

JOHN VAUXE

An East India Company Hostage Reflects Back upon the Siege
1691

Having gone to Surat to receive the farman (Document 18), Bombay's deputy governor John Vauxe found himself a hostage, along with much of the English factory, until the Company fulfilled its terms. He grew increasingly frustrated with his situation and expressed some of his views about the siege in letters to his father and brother, parts of which were then made public in England in an effort by critics to further discredit the Company. As a result of the letters, Vauxe was dismissed from the Company, both for his lack of discretion and for sending letters to England privately, which was forbidden by Company regulations. He remained at Surat, joining a long line of disgruntled former Company employees-turned-interlopers in the town. He drowned in 1697 when his boat capsized on the river near Surat. Vauxe's massive tomb, apparently paid for by his widow, was erected on the seashore nearby and appears on many old maps.

Mr. John Vauxe to his Father Mr. Thomas Vauxe in Bristol [England] dated in Surat [India] January the 22nd, 1691.

After it pleased God to take out of this world our General and Lieutenant General, it fell to my lot to take up the government and manage[ment] of the War, although besieged with an enemy of 25,000 men in close garrison having not above 300 Europeans and Topasses, which were hardly enough to manage our great Guns being 112 in Number and 5 Mortars. By often exercise [i.e., exchanging cannon fire] night and day [we] wasted and consumed much ammunition, which [was] soon found to grow low. Then we considered whether 'twas best to hold it out as long as men, money and ammunition lasted, then to acquit it [i.e., depart, presumably in the ships] and blow up the Fort. But in the meantime [we decided] to try, if there was any hopes of obtaining a peace from the

British Library, Add. MS. 22, 185, fols. 25–26.

Mughal [emperor], which we were encouraged from our vakil at Court would be granted if we sent up two sufficient Englishmen to the King's [i.e., Mughal emperor's] camp in an humble submissive manner and that [if] we would restore the merchants [who were] his subjects all that had been taken from them during the War, then [we had] hopes of a peaceable conclusion, which was put in agitation, and after some time effected. But not unless I would consent to remain hostage in the City of Surat until all was complied with according to the King's order, which on the 28th of February 1689 [i.e., 1690] I surrendered myself into their hands, where to this Day I remain, and know not when I shall get clear. Unless my masters will redeem me by some great person from Europe, here I must lie and be subject to thousands of abuses from the Moors, which grates hard against the grain of an Englishman.

But all is the sour fruits of war of which I have had an equal share of (with my Father) and shall all my days feel the smart of.

Mr. Vauxe to his brother Mr. Josiah Vauxe [January the 22nd, 1691] . . .

Our governor, lieutenant governor and all of the Council dying left no more commissioned officers that was of Council but myself to sit at [the] helm. But God be thanked at last we found an expedient and sent up to the Mughal's camp some messengers to treat on a Peace, which was effected after a blind manner, but not so much finished but that the Mughal required my person to lie in hostage, until all our agreements be complied with, which is not like to be otherwise until our masters [the East India Company] make due satisfaction for all injuries done his subjects. So that I am like to remain as I am [i.e., as a hostage] one, two or three years longer, which is most certainly greatly to my loss, and is now the occasion of my writing you from hence. If this be the fruits of war, let them that love it have their bellies full; for I have had fate bad enough in it.

7

The Company's War:
Defenders, Critics, Petitioners

20

JOSIAH CHILD

In Defense of the Company's War
1689

The Siege of Bombay was a matter of importance for commerce and politics in western India, but it also stoked controversies already raging in England over the East India Company. Sir Josiah Child, who more than any other was likely responsible for conceiving of and planning the war that prompted the Sidi's invasion, penned this revealing defense of the Company before he knew of the siege; he must, however, have been well aware that the recently returned East India ship Modena *(of which he was a principal owner) had not brought back any news of the much desired and expected farman and peace. Child was also one of late seventeenth-century England's most prolific economic theorists, and this pamphlet, like many of his writings, was intended both to defend his pragmatic interests in the Company as well as to further his more theoretical arguments on issues such as foreign trade, colonies, the nature of wealth, inflation, and so on.*

The Company have within the said seven years last past, so enlarged, and fortified the English fort of *St. George* and their city of *Madras*, upon the coast of *Coromandel*; that it is now one of the finest, and largest cities

---

[Josiah Child], *A Supplement, 1689. To a former Treatise, concerning the East-India Trade . . .* ([London], [1689]).

in those parts of the world, and secured by a good garrison, and containing at least one hundred thousand families of all nations, which inhabit within that city, and the territory about it, all subject to such laws for life and goods, as the Company by virtue of their charter think fit to impose upon them.

The customs and new impost paid His Majesty by the Company for two years, from *August* 1685 to *August* 1687 amounted to two hundred fifty thousand three hundred twenty six pounds, ten shillings and one penny, as by particulars presented his late Majesty [James II]. Since the Wars in *India*, it hath been less, by reason of those wars, but now the wars are over the Company's customs are like to be more yearly, than they were in either of the two years before-mentioned.

The Company have built new forts in, and otherwise, strengthened their Island of *Bombay*, and have ordered a dry dock to be built there, which they hope may be finish[ed] by this time, and all other conveniences for repairing and fitting the biggest English ships, and sent thither all stores needful for such purposes. . . .

And which is the most considerable national advantage, that ever was attempted by Englishmen in those parts of the world, the Company have reduced the principal part of their trade of *Surat*, to their own Island of *Bombay*; the inhabitants whereof from four thousand families, which they were computed at, when the Company first possessed that island, are since increased to fifty thousand families, all subject to the Company's laws. . . .

The *Mughal* being as is generally known, so great and powerful a Prince, it was vulgarly thought a vain or rather a distracted attempt in the Company to make any war upon him, as well in respect of his boundless riches, and power, as of the vast charges the Company should be at, in sending and maintaining warlike ships, into so remote parts of the world. Yet such hath been God's blessing upon the Company's arms, their unavoidable necessity, and their righteous cause, that that war beyond all men's opinion has ended to the eternal honor of the *English* Nation, in those parts of the world, and a peace concluded upon such honorable articles (the ratification whereof from the *Mughal* [emperor] himself in the *Persian* language are brought home now by the ship *Modena*) that if a blank had been delivered to the Company in *England*, to write down their own terms, they would not have desired more than is granted by the said articles. . . .

Now no nation in *India* hath such honorable terms with that great monarch, nor none so much respect from his governors in all places; which honorable and advantageous terms the *English* Company are like to enjoy for ages, because the former privileges the *English* had (which were never in any degree comparable to these) were only purchased by money from his great governors, and broke at their pleasure, when more money could not be got from other nations vying with us in trade, or *English* interlopers; whereas these are not only acquired by arms, and confirmed by the *Mughal's* own *farman* and *husb-al-hukum*,[1] but secured by maintaining a strong *English* garrison at *Bombay*, and making that island (which lies upon the principal parts of the *Mughal's* country, as the Islands of *Scilly* do upon *England*) the seat of the *English* dominion, and the center of their trade on the north coast of *India*, as *Batavia* is to the *Dutch East India* Company on the south. Which transition alone, from *Surat* to *Bombay*, could never have been done without a war as was beforesaid.

[1] "Husball Hoocombe" in original; an imperial decree made by the emperor or a deputy acting on his authority.

21

The Great Oppressions and Injuries Which the Managers of the East India Company Have Acted on the Lives, Liberties, and Estates of Their Fellow Subjects and Injustice Done to the Natives in Sundry Parts of India

1691

If figures like Josiah Child felt the war justified the East India Company's continued monopoly and power in England, many others, like the authors of this pamphlet, seized upon it as an example of its great failures. The great controversy over the East India Company was thus part of a much broader explosion of printing in late seventeenth-century England, which in turn intensified deeply political and economic debates on subjects like

A brief account of the great oppressions and injuries which the managers of the East India Company have acted on the lives, liberties, and estates of their fellow subjects, as also of their unjust dealings, not only with the adventurers themselves, but with the natives in sundry parts of India, whereby they have exposed the honor and interest of the [English] nation, and hazarded the entire loss of that advantageous trade. Humbly offered as reasons for establishing A New Joint-Stock (London, 1691).

*free trade and monopoly, monarchical and parliamentary power, the
structure of overseas trade and empire, and the relationship between
"public good" and "private interest." Ideas such as those found here, about
the Company specifically and the economy more generally, are echoed
in debates through the eighteenth century, up to and including Adam
Smith's* Wealth of Nations *(1776), a work often considered to mark the
birth of modern economic thought.*

VI. For procuring these unlimited arbitrary powers, which they have
exercised over their fellow subjects, they have expended great sums of
the Company's money, which stands charged in their books under the
title of *secret services*; besides the several 10,000 guineas which they did
present to the two late kings.

VII. Some of the prevailing members of the Committee have lately
introduced a new way of selling a very great part of the Company's
goods to themselves, by private contracts, to the great prejudice of the
usual buyers at their public sales, and so in few years have acquired vast
estate by defrauding all the other adventurers, contrary to their oaths
and the trust reposed in them.

VIII. They have not for many years past made up their books and val-
ued their stock, although by the general preamble, which is subscribed
by every adventurer at his admission to the Company, they stand obliged
to do [so] every seven years. Whereby the true value of the stock has
been concealed from the adventurers and all other persons, which
has given opportunity to the late managers to engross so great a part
thereof and to set up an uncontrollable absolute power in themselves for
carrying on their own *private designs*, in opposition to the interest of the
public, to the great oppression and damage of all those who have had
dealing with them, and of the adventurers themselves. . . .

IX. . . . [They have paid extremely high dividends, far exceeding their
receipts] by relation of which great and frequent dividends they have
not left a fund sufficient to carry on a trade of so large extent, and have
therefore been necessitated to farm it out to their fellow subjects under
the name of permission ships.[1] And not only so, but likewise to *Arme-
nians*, subjects to the King of Persia, which in time may be a means to
induce those people to import the goods of India in the shipping of that
country [Persia], as our laws allow them to do, and so will prove a very
fatal consequence to our navigation and trade. And further they have

---

[1]Some independent traders bought special licenses (permissions) from the Company
that allowed them to trade legally in Asia. Their ships were called permission ships.

permitted the *Jews* to establish themselves in India and have made them a part of their government there,[2] which in a manner has given them the entire possession of the diamond trade, to the great discouragement of the *English subjects*.

XI. Besides all these their arbitrary and illegal actions towards their fellow subjects, and their indirect proceedings to the prejudice of the joint-stock, their late dealings with the natives in India have also been unjust and scandalous, they having about six years past commenced an unjustifiable war with the Great Mughal, and under that pretense, committed many great depredations on the subjects of that prince, which has rendered the English in all parts of India odious and contemptible, and made them to be esteemed rather [as] pirates than [as] merchants; for they have made prize of the ships and goods of the natives to the amount of a million sterling, as appears by the depositions on record in their Majesties' Court of Exchequer. And they have also made assaults on the shore and destroyed by fire several houses, goods and ships, and have killed great numbers of the inhabitants; and as a further aggravation of their unjust proceedings, they have added a notorious breach of faith, by making prize of divers ships under the protections of the Company's passes; as also by seizing their goods and monies which were laden on freight, on board the Company's own ships, for which the bills of lading are still standing out. All [of] which outrages and depredations have been committed without any provocation to justify them. Nor did they ever make application to the Great Mughal for redress of those pretended grievances whereon they grounded their war against so great a prince, in whose dominions the subjects of England have always been received with the greatest marks of friendship and respect, and enjoyed greater privileges than any other Europeans, and beyond what the English have had in any other part of the world.

XII. . . . And now after they have by occasion of the said rash and unadvised war expended above £400,000 sterling, and lost above a million more [that would have gone] to the crown [in customs payments] and joint-stock by the interruption of their trade for several years past, they are at last become sensible of their unaccountable folly. And having submitted themselves by a humble acknowledgement of their faults, they have supplicated that great prince [the Mughal emperor Aurangzeb] for a pardon, which he, out of his accustomed clemency to the English nation, hath condescended to grant them, upon condition

---

[2]This may be a reference to Abraham Navarro, who had helped negotiate the peace (see Document 17).

that they restore what they have taken from his subjects, as appears by his farmans or patents, wherein their miscarriages are recorded to the great dishonor of this nation.

22

EDITH HOLLOWAY AND OTHERS

A Petition to the House of Commons by Widows of East India Company Sailors
1693

Sailors and their female kin were quite a politically active constituency, and they rather often petitioned Parliament and other bodies (including the East India Company) in the later seventeenth century. This petition reflects a dispute over lost wages and rights to "prizes"—that is, captured and confiscated ships and cargoes, in this case captured by the East India Company in its war with the Mughal Empire. Though this printed version does not bear Edith Holloway's name, an identical petition from a widow named Edith Holloway was read in the House of Commons on January 18, 1693. The House convened a committee to investigate the matter, but what came of it is unclear.

The East India Company, in the years 1683, 1684, 1685 and 1686, entered the said mariners on board several of their ships, to make direct voyages to and from the East Indies, *viz.* in the ships called The Charles the Second, the Beaufort, the Caesar, the Rochester, &c. and the said mariners were so taken on board in a merchant-like way, and at low wages, there being then no wars betwixt this crown and any Prince or state in the world. Nor did these mariners know of any war in India, nor did they any way apprehend any such thing was to be, when they proceeded in the said voyages.

The Case of the Mariners which Served the East-India Company in Their Wars in the East Indies and of the Widows and Orphans of Those That Perished in the Said Wars, to the Number of Five Hundred, and as Many Widows. Humbly Presented to the Honorable House of Commons (London, 1693).

That in some short time after their arrival in the Indies the Company's agents there engaged the said ships in an actual war against the Great Mughal and others, and by excessive tortures and punishment,[1] compelled the said mariners to serve in several places in their said wars, in several parts there on land very remote from any shore: yet the said agents found it absolutely necessary, not only by tortures, but also by many specious promises, for their encouragement, they should receive very great largesses [i.e., generous additions to their pay], more than their very low wages (as by law and in justice they ought to have) and thereupon they were, by the said Company's commanders, promised one full sixth part of all prizes that should be taken during the said war; which promises were put into writing, and publicly read in several of the said ships.[2]

That during the said war, there was taken in prizes to the value of £1,500,000 and upwards, proved in the [Court of] Exchequer, upon a bill brought by the Attorney General for the King's Tenths [i.e., the one-tenth of the value of a prize owed to the king], so that the sixth part belonging to the ships' companies amounts to about £260,000 and upwards.

That the said mariners have applied themselves from time to time to the said Company, for the said sum, or what should appear due to them, and were addressing themselves to this honorable House [of Commons] the last sessions for relief therein, whereupon a worthy member of this honorable House, and then Governor of the Company, promised the said mariners satisfaction if they would forbear; upon which promise they rested quiet, in sure hopes the same promise would be complied withal, which yet they have not done, but have most unconscionably offered such a small and inconsiderable sum as is not fit to be mentioned, which the said injured mariners have rejected, hoping, if they were entitled to such a sum, they are entitled to much more.

And forasmuch as this honorable House hath ordered the said Company to bring in their books, and a state[ment] of their debts and credits, the said oppressed mariners do humbly hope this honorable House will take notice, that they may have credit on the said Company's books for the said sum, in order they may have satisfaction for the same; and the rather, because in their answer to the Attorney General's bill, on the behalf of the King, they have set forth that the said mariners were to have a sixth part of all the said prizes. And further, for that the said

---

[1] Primarily flogging for disobeying orders.
[2] See Document 10.

prizes were converted to the use of the Company, and they [i.e., the Company leadership] have divided the same amongst themselves, and received the benefit of the same.

23

SHEIKH MAHMUD HOSSON, MULLA ABDUL GHAFUR, AND OTHERS

Surat Merchants, Clerics, and Port Officials Petition against the East India Company

1700

While people like Edith Holloway were challenging the Company in England, half a world away, others were pursuing much the same strategy with the Mughal government at Surat. In this petition, twenty-five prominent western Indian merchants, religious figures, and port officials seek help in recovering debts they claim were never repaid them, as promised by the Company, following the war and the Sidi's invasion. Like the Company's English enemies, they even go so far as to link the East India Company with the extraordinary increase in piracy in the Indian Ocean in the 1690s. Among the petitioners here was Abdul Ghafur, one of the wealthiest and most influential merchants and religious authorities in late seventeenth-century Surat and a longtime critic and commercial rival of the East India Company.

That in the time of Salabat Khan, Governor of Surat, one of the English Company's ships seized a ship of Abdul Ghafur's coming from Mocha hither. Upon notice thereof [the] said Abdul Ghafur complained to Salabat Khan, at which time Mr. [John] Child, a great villain, was President of the English Company who presently after got away from Surat and fled to Bombay. . . . [O]ut of his great clemency and love [the emperor Aurangzeb] did pardon them [the East India Company] and ordered the

British Library, India Office Records E/3/57 no. 7071, Copy of a Declaration or Demand of Several Merchants, 30 May 1700. (Persian version is at no. 7070.)

Sidi to quit Bombay. Then they requested a new farman to carry on their trade in Surat as formerly, which the Mughal [emperor] granted them.

During the space of one year the Company of English behaved themselves very civilly but then they began again to take and seize the merchants' ships of Surat and notwithstanding their agreement made before the Mughal [emperor] to deliver back all the ships' goods etc. taken by them, they shamefully and dishonorably put off the merchants from time to time for six years and upwards until the time of Amanat Khan [and] his coming [i.e., being appointed] governor of Surat, when they paid to several merchants some 30 percent, some 40 percent, and to some others (who in a manner forced them) 50 percent.[1]

But one year after they had made peace in I'timad Khan's time they took nine ships of Abdul Ghafur's and several other merchants' ships out of which they took the goods etc. and returned the empty hull. Again they also took [the] ship Ganj-i-sawai[2] belonging to the Mughal [emperor] within ten hours' sail of Bombay and delivered back the ship empty; they took also another ship full laden belonging to Hosson Hamdon [elsewhere, Ammadan]. Near Bombay [they] also [took] another ship laden belonging to Abdul Nabi, Secretary, and another also called the Quedah Merchant coming from Bengal to Surat, Hosson Hamdon's ship. And the Quedah Merchant they fitted up in order to commit further piracies which they kept [doing] on the coasts of Malabar. But hearing that their king was sending out some ships of war with some persons to do justice here they sold the two ships, since which they have committed no piracy. In this time the Company of English have robbed and taken from several merchants of Surat to the amount of eighty lakh[3] of rupees and have committed several villainies aboard the respective ships taken by them by which [they] have almost ruined the trade and port of Surat.

This that we have here declared we whose names are underwritten do swear to be true and now we hope and pray to God that we shall have justice done us.

[Letter signed by twenty-five prominent figures in Surat.]

---

[1] The Company allegedly reimbursed the merchants only a percentage of the full value of their ships and cargo.

[2] See also Document 24.

[3] A lakh is 100,000, so this would have been eight million rupees.

8

The Legacy and Memory of the Siege of Bombay

24

KHAFI KHAN

English Pirate Attacks and Continuing Tensions between Bombay and the Mughal Empire

1694

Relations between Bombay and the Mughal Empire remained tense and distrustful for a long time after the lifting of the siege, further aggravated by European pirate attacks on Mughal shipping. This document, originally written in Persian, describes a visit by its author to Bombay shortly after one such attack. This excerpt forms one small part of Khafi Khan's much longer, "unauthorized" history of the Mughal dynasty, and particularly of the reign of Aurangzeb, and focuses on an infamous incident involving the seizure of a Mughal ship by English pirates.

The royal ship called the Ganj-i-sawai, than which there was no larger in the port of Surat, used to sail every year for the House of God (at Mecca).[1] It was now bringing back to Surat fifty-two lakhs [i.e., 5,200,000] of rupees in silver and gold, the produce of the sale of Indian goods at Mocha and Jeddah. The captain of this ship was Ibrahim Khan. There

---

[1] The *Ganj-i-sawai* was a large ship that carried not only a great amount of goods and money, but a large number of pilgrims returning from the hajj (pilgrimage to Mecca).

Khafi Khan, *Muntakhab-al-Lubab*, excerpted in John Dowson, ed. and trans., *The History of India as Told by Its Own Historians* (London: Trübner and Co., 1877), vol. VII, 350–54.

were eighty guns and four hundred muskets on board, besides other implements of war. It had come within eight or nine days of Surat, when an English ship came in sight,[2] of much smaller size, and not having a third or fourth part of the armament of the Ganj-i-sawai. When it came within gun-shot, a gun was fired at it from the royal ship. By ill-luck, the gun burst, and three or four men were killed by its fragments. About the same time, a shot from the enemy struck and damaged the mainmast, on which the safety of the vessel depends. The Englishmen perceived this, and being encouraged by it, bore down to attack, and drawing their swords, jumped on board of their opponent. The Christians are not bold in the use of the sword, and there were so many weapons on board the royal vessel that if the captain had made any resistance, they must have been defeated. But as soon as the English began to board, Ibrahim Khan ran down into the hold. There were some Turkish girls whom he had bought in Mocha as concubines for himself. He put turbans on their heads and swords into their hands, and incited them to fight. These fell into the hands of the enemy, who soon became perfect masters of the ship. They transferred the treasure and many prisoners to their own ship. When they had laden their ship, they brought the royal ship to shore near one of their settlements, and busied themselves for a week searching for plunder, stripping the men, and dishonoring [i.e., raping] the women, both old and young. They then left the ship, carrying off the men. Several honorable women, when they found an opportunity, threw themselves into the sea, to preserve their chastity, and some others killed themselves with knives and daggers.

This loss was reported to Aurangzeb, and the news-writers of the port of Surat sent some rupees which the English had coined at Bombay, with a superscription containing the name of their impure King.[3] Aurangzeb then ordered that the English factors who were residing at Surat for commerce should be seized. Orders were also given to I'timad Khan, superintendent of the port of Surat, and Sidi Yakut Khan, to make preparations for [again] besieging the fort of Bombay. The evils arising from the English occupation of Bombay were of long standing. The English were not at all alarmed at these threats. They knew that Sidi Yakut was offended at some slights he had received. But they were more active than usual in building bastions and walls, and in blocking up the roads, so that in the end they made the place quite impregnable.

---

[2] This was the ship *Fancy*, captained by the English pirate Henry Every (or Avery).
[3] This was likely the "William and Mary rupee," struck at Bombay around 1692, with the names of the English monarchs, in Persian, appearing on the coin's obverse.

I'timad Khan saw all these preparations, and came to the conclusion that there was no remedy, and that a struggle with the English would result only in a heavy loss to the customs revenue. He made no serious preparations for carrying the royal order into execution, and was not willing that one rupee should be lost to the revenue. To save appearances, he kept the English factors in confinement, but privately he endeavored to effect an arrangement. After the confinement of their factors, the English, by way of reprisal, seized upon every Imperial officer, wherever they found one, on sea or on shore, and kept them all in confinement. So matters went on for a long time.

During these troubles I, the writer of this work, had the misfortune of seeing the English of Bombay, when I was acting as agent for 'Abdu-r Razzak Khan at the port of Surat. I had purchased goods to the value of nearly two lakhs [i.e., 200,000] of rupees, and had to convey them from Surat to 'Abdu-r Razzak, the faujdar[4] of Rahiri. My route was along the sea-shore through the possessions of the Portuguese and English. On arriving near Bombay, but while I was yet in the Portuguese territory, in consequence of a letter from 'Abdu-r Razzak, I waited ten or twelve days for the escort of Sidi Yakut Khan. 'Abdu-r Razzak had been on friendly terms with an Englishman in his old Hyderabad days, and he had now written to hint about giving assistance to the convoy. The Englishman[5] sent out the brother of his diwan,[6] very kindly inviting me to visit him. The Portuguese captain and my companions were averse to my going there with such valuable property. I, however, put my trust in God, and went to the Englishman. I told the diwan's brother that if the conversation turned upon the capture of the ship, I might have to say unpleasant things, for I would speak the truth. The Englishman's vakil [i.e., agent] advised me to say freely what I deemed right, and to speak nothing but the truth.

When I entered the fortress, I observed that from the gate there was on each side of the road a line of youths, of twelve or fourteen years of age, well dressed, and having excellent muskets on their shoulders. Every step I advanced, young men with sprouting beards, handsome and well clothed, with fine muskets in their hands, were visible on every side. As I went onwards, I found Englishmen standing, with long beards,

---

[4] A faujdar led a combined military and police force charged with keeping the peace in a particular area.

[5] This unnamed Englishman was probably Sir John Gayer, then governor of Bombay.

[6] A diwan was a revenue collector, who also served as a local or provincial governor, but could also refer more generally to a chief minister or adviser. In this case, it probably refers to a member of the Bombay council.

of similar age, and with the same accoutrements and dress. After that I saw musketeers, young men well dressed and arranged, drawn up in ranks. Further on, I saw Englishmen with white beards, clothed in brocade, with muskets on their shoulders, drawn up in two ranks, and in perfect array. Next I saw some English children, handsome, and wearing pearls on the borders of their hats. In the same way, on both sides, as far as the door of the house where he [i.e., Sir John Gayer, governor of Bombay] abided [i.e., lived], I found drawn up in ranks on both sides nearly seven thousand musketeers, dressed and accoutered as for a review.[7]

I then went straight up to the place where he [the governor] was seated on a chair. He wished me good-day, his usual form of salutation; then he rose from his chair, embraced me, and signed for me to sit down on a chair in front of him. After a few kind inquiries, our discourse turned upon different things, pleasant and unpleasant, bitter and sweet; but all he said was in a kind and friendly spirit towards 'Abdu-r Razzak. He inquired why his factors had been placed in confinement. Knowing that God and the Prophet of God would protect me, I answered, "Although you do not acknowledge that shameful action, worthy of the reprobation of all sensible men, which was perpetrated by your wicked men, this question you have put to me is as if a wise man should ask where the sun is when all the world is filled with its rays." He replied, "Those who have an ill-feeling against me cast upon me the blame for the fault of others. How do you know that this deed was the work of my men? By what satisfactory proof will you establish this?" I replied, "In that ship I had a number of wealthy acquaintances, and two or three poor ones, destitute of all worldly wealth. I heard from them that when the ship was plundered, and they were taken prisoners, some men, in the dress and with the looks of Englishmen, and on whose hands and bodies there were marks, wounds, and scars, said in their own language, 'We got these scars at the time of the siege of Sidi Yakut, but to-day the scars have been removed from our hearts.' A person who was with them knew Hindi and Persian, and he translated their words to my friends."

On hearing this, he [the governor] laughed loudly, and said, "It is true they may have said so. They are a party of Englishmen, who, having received wounds in the siege of [Sidi] Yakut Khan, were taken prisoners

---

[7] Sir John Gayer no doubt sought to convey an impression of strength at this critical juncture. However, these troop figures are clearly exaggerated.

by him. Some of them parted from me, joined the Habshi,[8] and became Muslims. They stayed with Yakut Khan some time, and then ran away from him. But they had not the face to come back to me. Now they have gone and taken part with the dingmars, or sakanas,[9] who lay violent hands on ships upon the sea; and with them they are serving as pirates. Your sovereign's officers do not understand how they are acting, but cast the blame upon me."

I smiling replied, "What I have heard about your readiness of reply and your wisdom, I have [now] seen. All praise to your ability for giving off-hand, and without consideration, such an exculpatory and sensible answer!" . . . I added, "What a manifest declaration of rebellion you have shown in coining rupees!"

He replied, "We have to send every year a large sum of money, the profits of our commerce, to our country, and the coins of the King of Hindustan are taken at a loss. Besides, the coins of Hindustan are of short weight, and much debased; and in this island, in the course of buying and selling them, great disputes arise. Consequently we have placed our own names on the coins, and have made them current in our own jurisdiction." . . .

The total revenue of Bombay, which is chiefly derived from betel-nuts and cocoa-nuts, does not reach to two or three lakhs [200,000–300,000] of rupees. The profits of the commerce of these misbelievers, according to report, does not exceed twenty lakhs [two million] of rupees. The balance of the money required for the maintenance of the English settlement is obtained by plundering the ships voyaging to the House of God, of which they take one or two every year. When the ships are proceeding to the ports of Mocha and Jeddah laden with the goods of Hindustan, they do not interfere with them; but when they return bringing gold and silver and ibrahimi and rial,[10] their spies find out which ship bears the richest burden, and they attack it.

---

[8] Habshi, meaning "Abyssinian," was another contemporary name for the Sidi, and possibly the origin of the term "Sidi" itself.

[9] Dingmars and sakanas were among a number of maritime peoples along the western Indian littoral.

[10] Gold and silver coins from Persia and the Middle East.

25

JOHN BURNELL

Bombay Twenty Years after the Siege
1710

Twenty years after the siege, the town, the fort, and the surrounding land-scape still bore many reminders of war but also signs of the Company's efforts to rebuild. John Burnell, another soldier in the employ of the Com-pany, offered his own description of the state of the island in a memoir he wrote about Bombay as it appeared to him around 1710. The memoir was not published until the early twentieth century.

The military of this Island consists of five companies of Christians, that is, Europeans, Topasses and Coffrees,[1] three whereof mount and relieve alternate[ly] in Bombay Castle, the eldest company being dis-tinguished by blue facings, the second green and the third red. The fourth company is wholly engarrisoned in Dongri [Fort], and the last in Mahim, Sion and Mazagaon, those two last forts being under the care of the commander of the First [Company], whose livery [i.e., uniform] is green faced with blue. Besides these forces are eight companies of sepoys,[2] seven of them containing eighty men each and likewise a suba-dar, hubladar, and a jumbladar or captain, lieutenant and ensign.[3] They have likewise two nayaks or corporals, they being all of them either Moors [i.e., Muslims] or Gentows [i.e., Hindus] of the Rajput caste. The eighth company consisteth but of ten men and an ensign. . . .

---

[1] These "Coffrees" were Madagascarians who were either military slaves or indentured military labor.

[2] A "sepoy" was an English rendering of the Persian and Hindustani word sipahi, or infantry soldier.

[3] "Hubladar" and "jumbladar" were the common English renderings of havildar and jamadar, both military officers. A nayak, in this instance, was the equivalent of a corporal or a captain.

John Burnell, *Bombay in the Days of Queen Anne, Being an Account of the Settlement.* Introduction and Notes by Samuel T. Sheppard (London: Printed for the Hakluyt Society, 1933), 10, 12, 19–21, 24–26.

The town of Bombay is divided into two distinct limits, the English and Black. The English town lieth to the southward of the Fort on a large spacious green, mostly straggling. It consists not of many buildings and those but of one story; the chief are the Deputy Governor's, before which is a large tank [i.e., an open-air water reservoir]. The barracks or soldiers' apartment is a very good foundation, in imitation of Chelsea College; it is of a great length, answerable in breadth, on each side whereof is a fine piazza supported with stone pillars; three apartments for commissioned officers, for the better ordering and keeping a good decorum among the soldiers, and a large room, on each side whereof run two long tables for them to diet at with decency, a bell to call them at meal times and several other conveniences. To it there belongs a barrack-master who is generally an ensign, and whose post is very beneficial.

[The Hospital and Burial Ground at Bombay]

Adjoining is seated the most famous European repository in the East, Mendham's Point, a name more terrible to a sick Bombaian than the Inquisition to a heretic: a cormorant paunch never satisfied with the daily supplies it receives,[4] but is still gaping for more, though it hath swallowed more English flesh than the Bengali Tamarind Tree, Madras Guava Garden, and the Green Hill at Bencala[5] yet still it hath room for those numbers twice told, and when those are digested it will be as ravenous as ever. . . .

[The burial ground] yields a most noble prospect as you lay in the road [i.e., offshore in a boat or ship], and is a great ornament to Bombay, containing above a hundred and forty large tombs, whereof twenty-eight have high spires, others pyramidical, and abundance built like summer houses with tomb tables in the center. The most remarkable are the Corkscrew, Capstern, and my Lady Gayer's tomb, first wife to Sir John Gayer, late General of India. It is a noble structure and takes up near a hundred foot square, having four gates and a handsome court before you enter the tomb, to which you ascend by steps. It is a hollow square within, the outside being embossed with pillars and cornish [i.e., cornice] work, the top covered with a cone surmounted with a pyramid and looks white as alabaster.

---

[4] The analogy is to the cormorant, a fish-eating bird said to be an especially voracious eater.

[5] These are all places of burial for the dead.

I had forgot the Shuffle Board Table,[6] under which lie the Company's writers. It is of a prodigious length, but I believe they have stopped its growing by looking out for themselves other apartments, not caring to consort like the soldiers, who lie there in rank and file, whole regiments of them. Their burial is but mean; neither are they allowed coffins; besides the jackals tear them out of their graves, burrowing in the ground like rabbits, to prevent which, they keep them down with rockstones, being all the sepulchres they have to their memory. Five ministers lie together in one tomb, four at the corners and one in the center, like the specks on a die. They have inscriptions cut in the chanam [i.e., plaster], neither is Latin or poetry wanting, each according to his fancy, some [tombs] having coats of arms, others weathercocks and sundials on them.[7] . . .

On the northern bounds of the Fort the hill continueth its length about a stone's throw, when it ends with a gentle descent. It is thickly covered all over with Moors tombs, the sepulchres of those who received their fate in the wars. They are brick, chamamed [i.e., plastered] over, of different forms, and lie directly north and south. . . .

The valley at the bottom of this hill is in the puckery[8] of Voll, being another part of the Company's estate. Here runneth in a small bill [i.e., promontory] and sandy bay, on the banks whereof is a place of interment and a cross erected, being as I have been informed the repository [burial place] of those soldiers who fell when Lieutenant Anthony Nangle[9] was drove back by the Sidi's forces, he losing then his ensign, Mr. Alexander Monroe, who was killed in this valley at the foot of Tomberree Hill [i.e., Mazagaon Hill], which here riseth with a steep ascent, its top being adorned with a multitude of palmero or brab trees. . . .

[The puckery of Parell in Sevdi is] a small town and hath adjoining a large noble convent, though now in ruins, belonging formerly to the Paulistins [i.e., Jesuits]. It is of a very good height and hath several large rooms and private apartments, with balconies and a broad staircase to ascend. The church is built of stone and makes one side of the square the convent is placed upon. It is very much decayed, the roof being wholly

---

[6] The allusion suggests a long flat slab of stone, here used to mark a collective grave for mid-level Company employees ("writers" were clerks or secretaries).

[7] The monuments were razed around 1764 because they were said to obstruct a clear line of cannon fire from the fort.

[8] A puckery (pakhadi) was an administrative subdivision or district, which was sometimes glossed in English as "parish."

[9] Burnell has the lieutenant's name wrong. It was Lieutenant Paine (according to Hilton).

fallen in, though some of the altarpiece is yet entire. . . . All the lands belonging to the convent (which were many and the most productive of any on the Island, extending from Sewri fort to that of Sion, upwards of four miles in length, including all the salt grounds) were seized on by the Company, who made themselves proprietors thereof, by reason that Padre Jose de Pandare in the late eruptions with the Sidi, was proved to have supplied the enemy with provisions and made over to the Sidi all the revenues of the church during his abode on the Island, as an encouragement to his arms to exterminate all the heretics[10] which were said to amount to a pound of gold a day. These and such other actions have forfeited all the right the Portuguese had to those lands which the Crown was pleased to grant them under the Great Seal, being allowed them by the favor of the English, and which they enjoyed till such time as their villainies were legible to the world; and then they were seized on by the General for the sole use and property of his masters. . . .

Cows are a scarce commodity on the Island, as in truth is everything else of provision [i.e., pertaining to food], we being beholden to our neighbors the Portuguese for almost everything that we eat; otherwise we might starve, were we only to subsist on the product of the Island.

---

[10] Kill the Protestant English.

A Chronology of the Siege of Bombay (1600–1709)

1600   English East India Company chartered by Queen Elizabeth I.

1602   The Dutch United East India Company (Verenigde Oost-Indische Compagnie, or VOC) created.

1616   English ambassador to the Mughal emperor Jahangir, Sir Thomas Roe, receives farman to settle an English factory and warehouse in Surat.

1658   Muhi al-Din Muhammad Aurangzeb (also known as Alamgir, or "world-seizer") becomes Mughal emperor.

1660   Charles II restored to throne of England and Wales, Scotland, and Ireland.

1661   Anglo-Portuguese alliance and marriage between the English king Charles II and the Portuguese princess Catherine of Braganza. Marriage treaty includes the transfer of the North African city of Tangier and the "Port and Island" of Bombay from Portuguese to English control.

1664   Maratha siege of Surat.

1668   Charles II grants the proprietorship of Bombay to the English East India Company.

1674   Sivaji Bhonsle crowned Maratha Chhatrapati (king or emperor).

1680–1707   Deccan (or Mughal–Maratha) Wars.

1681   Josiah Child serves first term as governor of East India Company in London.

1682   Dutch East India Company backs coup at Bantam (Banten) on Java, evicting English from the port.

1683–1684   English garrison soldiers and officers, led by Richard Keigwin, mutiny and take over Bombay for nearly a year.

1685 Accession of English king James II to the English throne.

1685–
1686 English East India Company decides to wage war against Mughal Empire and Siam.

1687 English East India Company announces the move of its western Indian headquarters (Presidency) from Surat to Bombay.

1688–
1689 English blockades of Mughal ports and seizure of ships of Mughal subjects (especially from Surat).

1689 *February 15* Sidi Yakut Khan invades Bombay.

March 11 Sambhaji Bhonsle, Sivaji's son and successor, executed by Mughal forces.

May 29 Three envoys sent from Bombay to negotiate peace terms.

1690 *February 4* Bombay governor John Child dies.

March 3 Word arrives that a peace has been agreed on, but negotiations continue with Sidi Yakut about the terms of the truce.

April 4 John Vauxe receives farman at Surat.

April 10 The fighting stops.

May 28 Official word reaches Bombay of the Revolution of 1688–89 (sometimes referred to as the "Glorious Revolution") that led to the ouster of King James II by the Dutch William of Orange and his wife Mary.

June 22 The last of the Sidi's troops, including some English deserters, depart the island.

1691–
1692 *December or January* James Hilton dies.

1695 Ship commanded by the pirate Henry Avery attacks *Ganj-i-Sawai*, a Mughal pilgrim ship returning from Mecca to Surat.

1698 "New" East India Company created in England.

1707 Death of Aurangzeb; union of England and Scotland to create Great Britain; death of Sidi Yakut.

1709 Old and New East India Companies merge to create United East India Company.

Questions for Consideration

1. What does the Bombay siege diary tell you about James Hilton? Why was it written and what do you think is missing? In what sense is it even a diary?

2. What do the actions and attitudes of the East India Company tell you about the nature of seventeenth-century companies? What are some similarities with and differences from corporations today?

3. What was daily life like in an early modern South Asian port town like Surat or Bombay? How did war affect that experience?

4. How did the Mughals and the East India Company conduct war both on land and at sea?

5. Why was the process of making peace between the East India Company and the Mughal Empire so drawn out and complex? How did each side regard the other?

6. How did the East India Company seek to "manage" ethnic and racial difference? When did these efforts work to calm conflict and promote loyalty, and when (or why) did they fail?

7. Some documents in this collection offer widely differing accounts of the same issue or event. Who is right?

8. How did conflict in the Indian Ocean affect the Company's reputation both in the British Isles and in South Asia?

9. What role did women play in relation to the East India Company and early modern economics and politics more generally? To what extent were they merely borne along by events beyond their control?

10. What long-term effects do you think the Sidi's invasion had on the East India Company, the colony of Bombay, and the British Empire?

Selected Bibliography

Alpers, Edward. *The Indian Ocean in World History*. New York: Oxford University Press, 2013.

Ames, Glenn. *Renascent Empire? The House of Braganza and the Quest for Stability in Portuguese Monsoon Asia, ca. 1640–1683*. Amsterdam: Amsterdam University Press, 2000.

Chaudhuri, K. N. *The Trading World of Asia and the English East India Company, 1660–1760*. Cambridge: Cambridge University Press, 1978.

Das Gupta, Ashin. *The World of the Indian Ocean Merchant 1500–1800: Collected Essays*. New Delhi: Oxford University Press, 2001.

Furber, Holden. *Rival Empires of Trade in the Orient, 1600–1800*. Minneapolis: University of Minnesota Press, 1976.

Gommans, J. J. L. *Mughal Warfare: Indian Frontiers and Highroads to Empire 1500–1700*. New York: Routledge, 2002.

Gordon, Stewart. *The Marathas 1600–1818*. Cambridge: Cambridge University Press, 1993.

Hasan, Farhat. *State and Locality in Mughal India: Power Relations in Western India, c. 1572–1730*. Cambridge: Cambridge University Press, 2004.

Kolff, D. H. A. *Naukar, Rajput, and Sepoy: The Ethnohistory of the Military Labour Market in Hindustan, 1450–1850*. Cambridge: Cambridge University Press, 1990.

Lawson, Philip. *The East India Company: A History*. London: Routledge, 1993.

Metcalf, Barbara D., and Thomas R. Metcalf. *A Concise History of India*. Cambridge: Cambridge University Press, 2002.

Nath, Pratyay. "Siege Warfare in Mughal India, 1519–1538," in Kaushik Roy, ed., *Warfare and Politics in South Asia from Ancient to Modern Times*. Delhi: Manohar, 2011.

Ogborn, Miles. *Indian Ink: Script and Print in the Making of the English East India Company*. Chicago: University of Chicago Press, 2007.

Pearson, Michael. *The Indian Ocean*. New York: Routledge, 2003.

Richards, John. *The Mughal Empire*. Cambridge: Cambridge University Press, 1996.

Steensgaard, Niels. *The Asian Trade Revolution of the Seventeenth Century: The East India Companies and the Decline of the Caravan Trade.* Chicago: University of Chicago Press, 1974.

Stern, Philip J. *The Company-State: Corporate Sovereignty and the Early Modern Foundation of the British Empire in India.* New York: Oxford University Press, 2011.

Strachey, Ray, and Oliver Strachey. *Keigwin's Rebellion (1683–84): An Episode in the History of Bombay.* Oxford: Clarendon Press, 1916.

Subrahmanyam, Sanjay. *Explorations in Connected History: Mughals and Franks.* New Delhi: Oxford University Press, 2005.

Subramanian, Lakshmi. *Ports, Towns, Cities: A Historical Tour of the Indian Littoral.* Mumbai: Radhika Sabavala for Marg Publications on behalf of the National Centre for the Performing Arts, 2008.

Watson, I. B. *Foundation for Empire: English Private Trade in India, 1659–1760.* New York: Vikas, 1980.

Index

Abd al-Allah (John Stevens). *See* Stevens, John
Abdul Ghafur (Abd al-Ghafur), 173–74
Abdul Hamid Lahori, 123
Abdul Nabi, 174
Abdu-r Razzak Khan, 177–78
Abyssinians. *See* Sidis
Acheen (Aceh), 98
Adil Shah, 127
Adventure (vessel), 74
Afghans. *See* Pathans (Pashtuns)
Ajmer, 125
Alamgir. *See* Aurangzeb, Emperor
āl-tamgah, 122. *See also* land tenure
Amanat Khan, 174
Amboyna Massacre, 7
Andrews, Jonathan, Captain, 35, 135
Anglo-Mughal War (First), 1–2, 3
  criticism of, 167–70, 171–73
  defense of, 166–68
  Mughal power and, 17–18
  regional and global context of, 9–13
  Revolution of 1688–89 and, 19–20
  ship seizures by Company, 12–13, 47, 135, 143, 171–73
  significance of, 23–24
  war aims of East India Company, 11–12, 139–41
Angre, Kanhoji, 19, 50*n*55
Annesley, Samuel, and Bartholomew Harris, "Diplomatic Overtures between Surat and the Company," 136–39
Ansley, Gowen, Captain, 29, 32, 42, 46
Anutt, Ramajee, 101
Ardis, William, 53, 103*t*
arrack, 68, 109
artillery, 87–88, 105, 145, 164. *See also* Siege of Bombay: artillery exchanges
  angle guns, 48
  battery ships, 37–39, 41, 48, 57–58, 103, 149
  culverins, 54, 83, 88
  damage to or accidents with, 37, 44, 60, 80, 82, 83, 86, 87, 102
  field, 30
  fire arrows, 96
  iron shells, 87, 94
  minion guns, 89
  mortars, 164
  partridge shot, 35, 35*n*23, 36, 82, 91
  placement of, 37, 39, 40, 51, 80. *See also* batteries, earthworks, and mines
  round shot, 51
  saker guns, 89

stern chaser, 44
stones shot from mortars or cannon, 60, 68, 69, 70–75, 77–80, 83–85, 87, 89
Asad Khan, 161–62
Aungier, Gerald, 8
Aurangzeb, Emperor, 3, 5, 9, 10, 11, 17, 97, 139*n*1, 170
  at a Chishti shrine, 125, 125*f*
  chronology, 184–85
  "Declaring a Peace? The Imperial Farman," 162–63
  Khafi Khan and, 126
  owner of *Ganj-i-sawai* pilgrim ship, 174, 175–76
  relations with East India Company 137–38, 139–41, 146, 157, 159, 173–74
Avery (Every), Henry, 176*n*2, 185

Babur, Emperor, 5
Bacherus, Johannes, 161
Bandareens (Bhandari). *See* soldiers (East India Company)
Bandora (Bandra), 58–59, 68, 152, 154
  Padre Superior of, 45, 45*n*46, 49, 58–59, 152. *See also* Jesuits
banians, 108, 152
Banten (Bantam), Java, 11, 184
Barber, Jacob, Captain, 34, 42, 52, 53, 62, 63, 67, 72, 74
Bardoly (Bardoli), 136, 137
Basra, 64
Bassein, 59, 98, 158, 159
Batavia (Jakarta), 78
Bathurst, Mr., 52, 83
batteries, earthworks, and mines, 21, 36, 56, 81, 88, 102, 103, 147, 151. *See also* artillery: battery ships
  cannon baskets (gabions), 82, 89, 103, 105
  Dongri Hill battery, 13, 34, 35, 36, 39, 100, 145, 151
  East India House battery, 39, 43, 145
  Ensign James' battery, 89, 93, 94, 96
  governor's house battery, 34, 36, 37, 39, 48, 66
  Moody's battery, 49, 52–53, 57, 68, 69, 77, 89, 91, 93, 100, 145, 149
  murchas, 84, 91, 92, 94, 96
  Mr. Harris's house battery, 88
  Nangle's battery, 65, 67, 73, 75, 77, 79, 80, 81, 103, 149, 151, 152, 153
  palmare wood used to reinforce, 14, 62, 67, 83–84, 87, 91, 92, 103, 105